PRAISE FOR THE BOOK

"I welcome this book as an invaluable resource, gleaning hard-won insights from exceptional yet unpretentious church musicians and ministers in nine congregations, Catholic and Protestant. On this basis, Kroeker develops themes that are vital to music and worship, the sound of which is good news for the future of church music."
—Frank Burch Brown, F.D. Kershner Professor of religion and the arts, Christian Theological Seminary, Indianapolis, IN

"By offering detailed accounts of the ways nine congregations have dared to enter brave and faithful pursuits of 'full, conscious, and active participation' in liturgy, this book invites us to consider evidence that all we have hoped worship might be is possible."
—Carol Doran, independent scholar and teacher

"What a gift to the church! This book highlights successful music programs that have impacted their congregations over a long period of time and describes the strategies musicians, clergy, and laity have employed to create mutually empowering relationships. Anyone involved in planning music and worship will find wisdom and encouragement in this helpful volume."
—Eileen Guenther, associate professor of church music, Wesley Theological Seminary, Washington, DC

"*The Sounds of Our Offerings* moves the ministry of music forward by providing concrete research into what makes a successful and enduring music program in a local church: clarity of theological vision, musical competency, commitment to collaborative ministry, and pastoral sensitivity to the people, all grounded in the liturgical vision of Vatican II."

—Kathleen Harmon, Music Director, Institute for Liturgical Ministry

"Discussions about church music have generated a lot of heat within American churches. At last, research has been conducted whose results shed light on this topic. Clergy and church musicians should devour *The Sounds of Our Offerings* and appropriate what they learn toward the good will and effective worship of their congregations."

—Terre Johnson, National Chair for Music in Worship, American Choral Directors Association

"The Sounds of Our Offerings is a welcome addition to the growing literature on the practice of church music in our day. A study of nine congregations of varying sizes and at various locales, the volume examines the patterns of leadership, use of resources, and exemplary practices marking communities recognized for their fine worship and music programs. Using a mixture of interviews of pastors and parish musicians and participant observation of worship in the communities, the researchers provide 'snapshots' of these communities' common public prayer. Of special interest is the focus on the theological and musical formation of pastors and musicians in each community as it affects their views on worship and worship music, their working relationship and the process of planning for worship, the role of the congregation in worship, and the relationship between resources invested and outcomes achieved."

—Michael Joncas, associate professor, University of St. Thomas, St. Paul, MN

"The Sounds of Our Offerings, with its widely diverse congregational case studies, provides a valuable resource for understanding the integral role of music in the experience of worship and the contribution

music brings to congregational revitalization. Kroeker has written an important resource for seminary education and continuing education for clergy."

—Nancy Ramsay, executive vice president, dean, and professor of pastoral theology and pastoral care, Brite Divinity School, Fort Worth, TX

"Charlotte Kroeker has given us exactly what we need: astonishingly good news about church music! Studying nine diverse congregations through a series of interviews, she poses keen, penetrating questions, eliciting insightful reflections from her subjects. What emerges is a sumptuous feast of 'best practices' that ought to be devoured by every clergy-person and church musician."

—William Bradley Roberts, professor of church music, Virginia Theological Seminary

"It is refreshing and enlightening to read a book in the important interdisciplinary area of church music and worship based upon field research revealing best practices. As a result of years of focused study, Charlotte Kroeker forms the right questions to probe *The Sound of Our Offerings*, and through this study of honest, faithful, applied practice, offers a snapshot of foundational areas and processes contributing to healthy music ministry."

—Tim Sharp, Executive Director, American Choral Directors Association

"Many churches are oases of health. Meaningful worship with well-conceived music marks their 'unremarkable' yet remarkable life together. Here are nine of their stories. Their profiles differ, and they do not give how-to prescriptions. They teach us the value of communal commitment to 'full, active, conscious participation.'"

—Paul Westermeyer, professor of church music, Luther Seminary

THE SOUNDS OF OUR OFFERINGS

THE SOUNDS OF OUR OFFERINGS

Achieving Excellence in Church Music

Charlotte Kroeker

ALBAN

Herndon, Virginia
www.alban.org

The Alban Institute
2121 Cooperative Way, Suite 100
Herndon, VA 20171

Unless otherwise noted, all Scripture quotations are from the New Revised Standard Version of the Bible, copyright © 1989, Division of Christian Education of the National Council of the Churches of Christ in the United States of America, and are used by permission.

Cover design by Tobias Becker, Bird Box Design
Cover image: Stained Glass Ceiling at Palau de la Música Catalana in Barcelona by Carlos Lorenzo
Rural Arkansas church photographs by David Mann. Reprinted with permission.

Library of Congress Cataloging-in-Publication Data

The sounds of our offerings : achieving excellence in church music / [edited by] Charlotte Kroeker.
    p. cm.
Includes bibliographical references (p. 233).
ISBN 978-1-56699-395-1
1. Music in churches. 2. Church music. 3. Music--Religious aspects--Christianity. I. Kroeker, Charlotte Yvonne.
ML3001.S68 2011
264'.2--dc23
                                    2011023696

11   12   13   14   15   VP   5   4   3   2   1

Contents

Foreword

EXCELLENCE IN CHURCH MUSIC IS NO EASY MATTER these days. Achieving and sustaining faithful and relevant music in churches is like sailing a ship with precious cargo into heavy seas. The cultural, religious, and market-driven crosscurrents are strong, and the winds of fashion are unpredictable. From my observations as a church musician for half-a-century involved in multiple Catholic and Protestant contexts—seminars, workshops, convocations, and retreats—it is a joy to encounter singing congregations who are gracefully led into vital, faithful, and relevant musical liturgy.

The good news of this book is that there are remarkable church music programs despite all the pressures and obstacles to excellence. Making integrated decisions about music in local assemblies requires musical talent, vision, skill, pastoral sensitivity, and a sustained love of shaping the life of faith by ordered sound. By a careful study of nine congregations, this book shows how this is so. There is rich diversity among the three Catholic, three Presbyterian, and three Episcopal churches we meet in these pages. Their stories will give hope to many who are wrestling with these issues. The healthiest places show simultaneous appreciation for the deeper traditions in which they stand and for true ecumenical sharing of theological insight and musical sensibility.

Even more, these are not "blockbuster" overnight sensations. Rather, we are given access to the persons and skill sets that make musical excellence in worship and congregational life happen. The research represented here take us "behind the scenes" as it were. What kind of leadership is required? What styles of collaboration really work? What are the visions of faithful musical liturgy found in these places? What are the varied planning processes? What views of congregational participation emerge? What kind of relationships between pastors, musicians, and the assembly contribute to the impressive achievements these congregations have made?

Those are the questions traced in this book. Of course the readers will recognize that certain theological convictions are shared as well. The influence of the best of Vatican II and its non-Roman translations are part of the pulse at the heart of these studies. Each of the authors was looking for what Robert Hovda once named "strong, loving, and wise" worship. We can see in these pages that this is in fact possible in a wide variety of demographics.

My hope is that this study will provoke readers to undertake such questions and investigations in their own congregational contexts. The stories are here and they are real. What remains is the challenge of looking for analogies and common elements in how each congregation, each pastor/musician combination can deepen over time the "sounds of our offerings" to God, for the sake of the Gospel and the world.

Don E. Saliers
Wm. R. Cannon Distinguished Professor of Theology
  and Liturgy, Emeritus
Emory University

Preface

THIS BOOK OFFERS GOOD NEWS ABOUT THE MUSIC OF the church. It recounts what has been learned from studying nine congregations where music has garnered the full, conscious, active participation of the people over a significant period of time. The book probes how these churches have built music programs that have lasted, what is responsible for this good news, and who and what make it happen. We asked pastors and musicians to reflect on their work together and were rewarded with rich insights and honesty about what does and does not work. We asked volunteer musicians, professional musicians who offer their skills as church members, and other members of congregations about their experiences with music in worship. We visited worship services, looked at budgets and instruments, and ascertained the abilities of the volunteer musicians in these churches. No site was without its struggles and difficult situations, yet these congregations are successful in achieving meaningful music for worship. A view of a rich tapestry of music in worship across the United States is the result.

The music choices in these churches are not restricted to a particular style, but rather reflect the accumulated repertoire that is meaningful to the congregation, along with new music members are discovering for their worship. We encountered no changes in leadership that initiated turnaround miracles. Rather, we found what some may describe as unremarkable, week-to-week, year-to-year, faithful rendering of "better" music for prayer and praise. When the music program took a slightly different turn, the new adventure was built on the foundations of the past.

This book is not a prescription for "success." It is not a sociological study of music in congregations based on statistical data (though we consulted such studies in devising the research plan). It is not a psychological study of effective leadership styles or of personalities most likely to win musical friends or populate church pews. We did not discover the one type of priest or musician with the education or background most likely to succeed in parish work. Some may even conclude that we were elitist about the churches we chose. (We admit that we wanted the best music programs we could find, though geographical location, demographics, size, and financial resources vary greatly among the churches.)

Rather, these are the stories of churches with reputations for their exceptional music programs, churches that have built these programs in consistent, coherent ways. These nine models demonstrate how music can serve as a vehicle to carry a congregation's prayer and praise effectively. In all cases, the music programs span multiple priests or pastors and musicians, an indication that the music programs have found their way into the life and faith practices of the congregations. Despite some marked differences, common characteristics of these effective music programs that can be replicated are worthy of mention and celebration.

Through the Eyes of Vatican II

At the foundation of all the music programs of these churches are two principles grounded in the documents coming from the Second Vatican Council. The reforms of Vatican II that began in the 1960s not only changed the nature of worship in the

Catholic Church but also spilled over into worship practice in nearly all Christian faith traditions. Conversely, as the Catholic Church made the transition to liturgy in the vernacular and needed music with English texts, it borrowed extensively from Protestant riches. The U.S. Conference of Catholic Bishops recognized the need for liturgical scholarship and established centers to fill this need, including one at the University of Notre Dame. Scholarly work in liturgy in the Catholic Church encouraged scholarship in other faith traditions as well, and particularly those represented in this study.

Unfortunately, scholarly work in the history and practice of church music did not follow the scholarship in liturgy. Rather, music was allowed to follow its own path without the attention or scholarly rigor the church gave to liturgy. With a rich history of music developed over hundreds of years, Catholics suddenly were thrust into an era in which their sacred Latin texts were replaced by texts in the vernacular for the "full and active participation by all the people," as stated in the *Constitution on the Sacred Liturgy (CSL)*. Although change was not so abrupt in other Christian traditions, the Vatican II changes gradually affected worship practices across denominations. These new musical practices were rarely grounded in theological or musical reflection, and certainly were not afforded the care given to liturgy by scholars.

Nevertheless, church music composition blossomed wherever there was need or inspiration and gave rise to a great period of experimentation and the sharing of repertoire across faith traditions. At the same time, the secular music publishing houses filled practical needs, unhampered by the long processes required to produce approved hymnals and providing stiff competition for denominational publishing houses. Denominational publishers could no longer depend on the loyalty of congregations as the motivation to buy their publications, sometimes even where the denomination's own hymnal was concerned. The excitement generated by this experimentation in music was accelerated by publishers eager to capture new markets. The benefit was a wealth of new music for the church; the downside was a loss of means for discerning the quality and use of the music. A major shift had occurred: the marketplace now profoundly determined the way music found its way into the church. For Catholics, the well-thought documents of the *Constitution on the Sacred Liturgy* were never really applied and Protestants were at times eager to abandon their own long-standing traditions to try new music. The result? Supply and demand economics prevailed in an era of great societal and cultural change. A bounty of new sacred music found its way into Christian worship whether or not the denomination had screened its theological integrity, musical quality, or determined its appropriateness for liturgy.[1]

CSL affirms the importance of music "as sacred song closely bound to the text, forming a necessary or integral part of the solemn liturgy." *CSL* calls for genuine art to be admitted into worship. The treasure of sacred music is to be preserved and fostered with great care. Choirs are to be developed. Importance is placed on the teaching and practice of music in seminaries and other Catholic institutions. Chant is to be maintained. The pipe organ is to be esteemed. Composers are to be encouraged to develop sacred music, especially as a vocational pursuit.[2]

Hearing the text of the Catholic documents, one of the Protestant pastors interviewed said, "Why, that sounds as if it is describing Protestant worship practice!" Both Episcopal and Presbyterian documents, though worded differently and perhaps not as comprehensive, agree with the importance and function of music in liturgy. For example, a 1980 Episcopal manual for clergy and church musicians states:

> From the early days of the Church, music has been integral to the worship of God. Music gives solemnity, beauty, joy, and enthusiasm to the worship of the community. . . . It shall be the duty of every Minister to see that music is used as an offering for the glory of God and a help to the people in their worship. . .[3]

From Presbyterian sources, we learn: "The arts, especially music and architecture, contribute to the praise and prayer of a Christian congregation. . . ."[4] And this: "Song is a response which engages the whole self in prayer. Song unites the faithful in common prayer wherever they gather for worship whether in church, home, or other special place."[5]

Vatican II goals for music and liturgy, to promote the "full, conscious, active participation" of the people and for music to form "a necessary and integral part of the solemn liturgy," frequently have been adopted by non-Catholic Christian denominations. These two criteria were used to choose the nine congregations described in this book.[6]

Nature of the Study

This study has its roots in a 1999 interdisciplinary conference, "Church Music: Looking Back into the Future," funded by the Louisville Institute. The conference identified two specific issues that relate to this project:

1. The need to address issues of music within the environment where it is practiced—that is, as a part of a greater whole, where priest/pastor, musician, and laity are all contributors to the process; and
2. the need to understand the resources necessary for vital worship.

In January 2005, a consultation in Louisville was convened by seminary and church musician Carol Doran and her colleague Bill Roberts, "Equipping Pastors to Use Music to Revitalize Congregations," where participants created a statement calling for the exploration of ways that pastors and musicians share the work of creating liturgy and music for worship. This study addresses the issues raised in both the 1999 and 2005 gatherings.

While a community of scholars is one important starting point for such a study, the other is the local parish. The goals and values of church documents remain merely ideas if their practical implementation is impossible. This study attempts to further enlarge the relatively small body of research available on the music of congregational worship practice and to give examples of how Vatican II's noble ideals for music are reflected in the practice of nine congregations.

The congregations we studied were chosen with pragmatic considerations in mind. While churches of various sizes were included, their locations were chosen for proximity and accessibility to the researchers. "Successful" music programs were chosen in light of researchers' knowledge of churches in their respective geographical areas or that of colleagues who said, "You should study that church. It has a great music program!"

Three Catholic, three Episcopal, and three Presbyterian congregations comprise the study. Located in the Northwest, Southwest, Midwest, and Northeast, the churches represent inner-city, suburban, and urban locations, and range in size from seventy-five to thousands of members.

The study investigates the leadership and resources for liturgy in local parishes where music is a vital part of the worship life. We probed what resources contribute to such worship, how leaders of worship think about what they do, and how they decide what works and what doesn't. Through this process, we uncovered exemplary practices and sought to describe systems for those who seek to make music in worship more effective. While our near-term goal is to provide information and analysis that will help leaders effectively implement music in liturgy, our ultimate goal is to strengthen and deepen the voice of the faithful in their praise and prayer to God.

In our research, we examined the characteristics of the leaders, the organizational planning processes, the available resources, and the relationships between these facets of leadership. To ensure that we would study a diverse group of congregations, we focused on the following criteria:

1. Variety in location: For example, we have included a suburban church with many resources, a cathedral in a declining neighborhood, an integrated/mixed-race parish, and an older urban/low-income parish.
2. Ecclesial characteristics: For example, sites with a single priest/minister, cathedrals with multiple clergy and musicians, and churches with parochial schools.

Most important, we explored the extent to which the churches fulfilled the fundamental values of Vatican II as embraced in each denomination. Because the music of Christian worship and the musicians who make that music regularly cross denominational lines, we found points of comparison and contrast between denominations as music was offered in liturgical practice.

First, we focused on the nature of leadership and the planning processes for worship. We discovered how clergy, musicians, and lay leaders thought about music in the liturgy. We watched congregations at worship. We listed and analyzed the resources used, including the traditions of the parish.

Then we described the "lenses" through which the congregations viewed worship, how resources were used, what assumptions about worship prevailed, and how they were implemented.

We probed what the priest/minister and musician brought to their jobs—their educational backgrounds, motivations for doing their work, how they understood their work (as a calling/career/job), what mentors influenced them, their perceptions of parishioners' musical abilities, and their understandings of the role of music in worship.

We asked what resources were available for planning, such as indices, sacramentaries, liturgical aids, hymnals, lectionaries, and published planning guides. (Readers seeking more information or resources are directed to www.churchmusicinstitute.org.) We asked what educational and human resources were available—such as a local university, music libraries, and publisher-sponsored workshops. We asked what instruments were on site and how they were maintained and upgraded. We determined the annual budget for music and liturgy when that information was available to us. We asked how the church was involved in hosting community musical events or in taking music into the community. We described the nature of the space for worship. We asked what opportunities staff members were given for continuing education and reflection.

We probed how planning was done, both formally and informally. We asked how the musicians and priests/pastors saw their own roles and that of the other in making decisions. We inquired what happens when something goes wrong. We asked if there was a mechanism to solicit regular feedback or input from the laity.

Each pastor and musician was interviewed individually, with the researcher using the questions in appendix A. Then the researcher attended worship services to observe the liturgy in action. A second interview with pastor and musician followed, based on the questions in appendix B. We later returned to the interviewees to ask questions about congregational perspectives, listed in appendix C. In some cases, we were able to speak with the chair of a worship or liturgy committee. In one case, we had access to the results of a congregational survey that included questions about music. In other cases, we spoke individually with congregational members, choir members, or parents of young children to ask about their experiences of music in the church. The limits of the study precluded formally studying congregational perspectives other than observing worship and conducting informal conversations. Thus, we focused instead on the leaders of music in the church. Beyond these initial points of contact, subsequent visits and conversations broadened our understanding of each site.

Three Denominations,
Nine Churches, Nine Contexts

Three Catholic parishes were included in the study:

1. An urban cathedral in the West (chapter 1) reflects the diverse ethnicities of its community. This remarkable congregation transformed an unwieldy building in a declining area of a city, creating a beautiful worship space where a program of music and arts now nurtures the worship of a growing and eclectic congregation, driven by the leaders' vision of the power of the arts to carry theology.

2. A large suburban parish church in the Upper Midwest has an attached school (chapter 2); the growth of the music program has been integral to the growth of the parish and school.

3. In a small, urban "parish of choice" in the Upper Midwest, some of whose parishioners travel to church from great distances (chapter 3), the liturgy is offered by a long-standing musician, part-time priests who have had musical training, and a congregation that takes ownership of the liturgy through a committee that shapes nearly every aspect of the liturgical life of the church.

We also explored three Episcopal churches:

1. A parish church in a Midwest suburb (chapter 4) has embraced the riches of Anglican music traditions and reaches for and achieves transcendence in worship.

2. A parish church in a New England suburb (chapter 5) is an ethnically and socioeconomically diverse congregation whose worship is driven by a social-justice ethos, .

3. An inner-city, East Coast cathedral church (chapter 6) is being transformed by the parish's investment in an attached music school that brings together talented children of wide diversity for training and for service to the liturgy and the community.

The Presbyterian churches (Presbyterian Church [USA]) are all in the Southwest:

1. A midsize church in a Southwest university town (chapter 7) places great importance on its music program and gives scholarships to university music students who enrich congregational worship.
2. In a church in an urban neighborhood (chapter 8), the investment in a strong music program is mirrored by investment in social-outreach programming.
3. An inner-city church in a changing neighborhood (chapter 9) supports a music program that is vital to the spiritual identity of the many aging members of the church.

Summary of Findings

This book summarizes findings that are common to denominations and contexts (chapter 10), looking especially at these factors:

1. *The theological and musical formation of the pastor and the musician.* In each site, we sought to learn how both pastor and musician were formed theologically and musically, what childhood experiences (including family and church influences) and mentors influenced their formation, and what educational experiences prepared them for their current work.

2. *How the musical, theological, and educational formation of pastor and musician contributes to their ways of working together.* We explored the extent to which they function in totally

different domains, work with some understanding of each other's domain, or share a significant knowledge of music and theology that allows ease in communication.

3. *Views of pastor and musician on theology and music in liturgy.* We tried to understand how the pastor and musician think about music in worship and how these views affect their worship planning. We tried to determine the degree of empathy between pastor and musician—their common goals, vocabulary, and understandings, and the differences they must address.

4. *Nature of the working relationships and planning processes.* We asked each pastor and musician how their individual tasks combine to create liturgy. Who does what? How is music chosen? When is there conflict? How is it resolved? What role does personality play in their ability to work together?

5. *Role of the congregation in liturgy.* We observed the congregation's participation in worship, noting worshipers' level of involvement in singing, the nature of the singing they were asked to do, and the division of singing between leadership (cantor/choir) and congregation. We tried to determine how the congregation gave feedback about music for liturgy. We asked questions of congregational members or chairs of worship/liturgy committees when possible.

6. *How do the leaders consider the perspective of the congregation when choosing music for worship?* How do they define "participation"? How do they determine the congregation's musical abilities so they can choose appropriate music for worshipers to sing?

7. *Relationship between resources invested and outcomes achieved.* How are music expenses funded, and to what extent are they funded through an annual budget? Is there a correlation between the dollars invested and the attainment of goals?

8. *Nature of congregation's response to pastor-initiated musical change when the musician has been in place for a longer period of time than the pastor.* How does that affect congregational

singing, the musician's decision-making, and the relationship between the new pastor and the musician?

We acknowledge that our study of these nine parishes offers only a snapshot of the rich landscape of churches across America.[7] All of the researchers and undoubtedly our readers know many more congregations that could contribute substantively to such a study. Yet this research project has provided opportunity to probe the inner workings of positive worship and music practices in nine churches with much to share. These are their stories.

Photographs of Rural Arkansas Churches

Arkansas photographer David R. Mann has provided visual companions to the sounds of our offerings in worship with the images of rural churches included in this book. Old country churches with their hardwood floors and straight back benches were the perfect places to sing. The acoustics were live, the posture of the singers was erect, and an acoustic upright piano provided ample accompaniment for enthusiastic singing. As Pulitzer Prize-winning journalist Paul Greenberg says of these Arkansas photographs, ". . .the old churches still live. And call to us, as in call-and-response, the traditional refrain of the black church."[8]

The churches where the congregations of this book worship look very different from these photographs. Yet the current churches have live acoustics, good seats for singers, and effective accompaniment for congregational singing. The fundamentals of music for worship have not changed. These congregations are connected with their roots, knowing from where they have come, their past informing their present and future. Simple truths underlie their communal lives of faith that continue from generation to generation, similar to the worshippers in these rural churches.

Paul Greenberg continues, "Each picture is a simple gift. As in the Shaker hymn, 'Tis the gift to be simple, 'tis the gift to be free, 'Tis the gift to come down where we ought to be. . .There is something about these pictures that says: This is where you ought to be. Something that says: Be still."

And so it is when we recognize a melody in a hymn or anthem—it reminds us of a faith experience, a moment with God, a sacred milestone of life shared with friends and family; it brings back a text that offers hope and renewal. Just like these photographs, the music calls us. We are still. We listen.

David Mann, the artist, says of the rural church of his family in Texas that inspired this project, "I have visited and photo-graphed the church numerous times and if I close my eyes and listen, I can almost hear the piano, the singing, and preaching, which echoed off the wood-plank walls for so many years. I know that many Arkansans have a similar church or institution in their family history and I hope that these photos inspire viewers to think about, research, or visit that physical or spiri-tual place in their past."[9]

The sounds and places of our offerings connect us with our spiritual being and ultimately with God. That is why they de-serve our care and keeping, not as objects of our worship, but as reminders of the holy. As we respect and understand these precious gifts, it is then they will carry our best worship to God.

Charlotte Kroeker

Acknowledgments

THIS STUDY COULD NOT HAVE TAKEN PLACE WITHOUT the faith, vision, encouragement, and financial support of Betty Van Gorkom and Mario and Mary Kay Pasin, who repeatedly took time for conversations that shaped the project. Mrs. Van Gorkom provided initial funding, and Mr. and Mrs. Pasin provided continuing resources to make certain the study could accomplish its purpose. I cannot thank them enough. I am also grateful to the Institute for Church Life (ICL) at the University of Notre Dame, where this project began, to those who completed the Notre Dame Study of Catholic Parish Life after which this one is patterned, and to Ginny Nawrocki at ICL, who efficiently handled many details. Additional thanks go to Jean Ann Linney of the provost's office, who provided forward motion at a critical juncture for the project. For the support of my colleagues Craig Cramer and Gail Walton (1954–2010), I am profoundly grateful.

My co-researchers Annette Conklin and Linda Clark have contributed vitally to the structure, data, writing, and evaluation of the data. Linda's earlier research in congregational worship and consultation in preparing the research model, along with that of James Davidson of Purdue, was invaluable. Annette's fine musicianship could always be counted on to inform the process, and her Catholic formation gave insights that this Protestant would certainly have missed. Both Annette's and Linda's on-site research broadened the reach of the study. Richard Conklin's careful reading of the manuscript and use of his red pen mean that the ideas of the book cross denominational and intellectual boundaries with greater ease. I thank him for challenging my ill-wrought arguments and sharpening the better ones. Despite the profundity these contributors have given the text, the ultimate responsibility for its shortcomings is mine.

I want to thank Ernan McMullin (1924–2011) and John Roche for allowing me to be their student of interdisciplinary scholarship. Though both work in the field of science and religion (among others), they helped me to understand the importance of respecting individual disciplines and combining them with integrity. Further, I am indebted to the writings of Ernest Boyer for introducing the scholarship of application, and to his wife, Kay Boyer, for giving insights into his life and work that added depth to his writings.

A good friend of Ernie Boyer, Harold McGraw (1918–2010), understood the importance of these ideas in helping launch the Church Music Institute (CMI) in 2006, along with Anne Stewart, Jeanne Johnson, and Kim and Diana Warner. I am appreciative of the CMI governing board, which allowed me time to do the writing necessary to complete the project. My parents, Wesley and Dolores (1923–1989) Kroeker, taught me the importance of singing the faith from my earliest memories. Piano teachers Ava McDaniel, Virginia Wheeler, Kenneth Mays, Eugene Ulrich, and Robert Edwards all served the church in addition to being piano professionals. Robert Laughlin set a standard and gave a lifetime responsibility when he said whatever I did would be done well. Wilma McKee taught me how to combine music with worship for campfire services in my teens. Mary Ellen Sutton gave me thorough foundations for playing the organ, especially leading congregational hymns from the organ, and forever changed my soul with J. S. Bach's organ works.

Time spent in Jerry Hilton's study preparing worship started this current journey. Jim and Wanda Cowles helped to clarify what is most important in life and work. To my husband, Robert Mann, I give deepest thanks for reading and editing drafts, putting up with my working at all hours, and cooking meals I did not deserve.

Finally, I thank the staff of the Alban Institute for taking a chance on a book about church music, and editor Beth Gaede for always staying with me until we found a way to say what needed to be said. I am grateful. Most of all, thanks must go to those who provide profound and beautiful vehicles for liturgy and music for worshiping congregations, even when unnoticed and unrewarded, but who consistently provide the means for these congregations' vibrant liturgy, the work of the people.

Introduction

I OFTEN SAY THAT CHURCH MUSICIANS ARE SOME OF THE most centered, sincere people I encounter, because no one goes into church music for the wrong reasons. Job security, power, and prestige are not usually high priorities for those considering a career in church music. Likewise, the study of church music has not attracted research dollars proportional to the effect it has in our society. Prestigious music schools are largely secular institutions. Seminaries rarely teach church music courses, and churches, clergy, and musicians are left for the most part to sort out on their own how music works.

Denominational organizations offer practical workshops and repertoire sessions for church musicians, but reliable research in the field of church music is rare. In some ways, this state of affairs is not surprising. Higher education in the United States is defined by disciplines, and church music is interdisciplinary, involving both music and theology. Seminaries and music schools where clergy and musicians are trained rarely exist in proximity to each other. Add another dimension to music and theology, the involvement of the congregation—how can church music have meaning unless the congregation is vitally involved?—and the reasons church music is rarely studied begin to emerge. Church music is a complex entity by its multidisciplinary nature, and those who might study it, professors of theology and of music, are professionally removed from each other. While musicians and theologians may be uncomfortable venturing beyond their own fields of expertise, exploring how congregations function is likely yet another step beyond their comfort zone. But the worship of God is central to Christianity, and understanding how to do worship well is a worthy endeavor.

Building on the Work of Ernest Boyer

The work of Ernest Boyer can be helpful for understanding how the research in this book about church music fits into the larger landscape of research in general. In 1990, Boyer, then the president of the Carnegie Foundation for the Advancement of Teaching, wrote *Scholarship Reconsidered: Priorities of the Professoriate,* a book that was to dominate much of the conversation about higher education for the next decade. In this book Boyer raised questions about the way scholarship was defined and, ultimately, opened thinking about what constitutes "research." The four categories of scholarship Boyer introduced are important to understanding the work of this book.

The scholarship of discovery is perhaps the most familiar category, at least to those acquainted with higher education, and is what we generally mean by "research." This category refers to the pursuit of "knowledge for its own sake, to freedom of inquiry and to following, in a disciplined fashion, an investigation wherever it may lead. It not only means the discovery of new ideas, but the process of thinking, the meaning of outcomes, the excitement of pressing into the unknown."[1] This research uncovers new facts, proposes new ideas, and charts new territory, such as discovering a vaccine for polio (saving millions of lives) or uncovering a lost manuscript of Bach (changing how we view the history of music).

The scholarship of integration focuses on "making connections across the disciplines, placing the specialties in larger context, illuminating data in a revealing way, often educating nonspecialists, too. . . . serious, disciplined work that seeks to interpret, draw together, and bring new insight to bear on original research." Research in integration is done at the boundaries where fields converge.[2] This research creates a new entity out of two formerly separate ones.

While the scholarship of discovery and integration involves the investigation and synthesis of knowledge, *the scholarship of application* asks different questions: "How can knowledge be responsibly applied to consequential problems? How can it be helpful to individuals as well as institutions?"[3] Or, how does what we have learned from discovery and integrative research affect real-life situations in practical, meaningful ways? Further, how can the acquisition of this knowledge give rise to service, to the betterment of the larger world?

The scholarship of teaching grows out of the idea that knowledge has no function if it cannot be transmitted to others. "Teaching begins with what the teacher knows. Those who teach must, above all, be well informed and steeped in the knowledge of their fields." Further, "teaching is also a dynamic endeavor involving all the analogies, metaphors, and images that build bridges between the teacher's understanding and the student's learning . . . great teachers create a common ground of intellectual commitment . . . they stimulate active, not passive, learning."[4] Good teachers not only know their own field well, but they are just as excited about others' engagement in that field and welcome them into the joy of learning. Knowledge worth transmitting to future generations is worthy of thoughtful pedagogy.

Boyer's categories are helpful for an understanding of the nature of church music in that we are studying two discrete fields, music and theology, as they are combined to create a new interdisciplinary entity for worship. Further, when we study how music and theology function as a vehicle to carry the praise and prayer of the people in worship, we are studying the application of this new, interdisciplinary entity. Then, as we probe how the effective practice of music and liturgy can be transmitted to new generations of worshipers, we are delving into a scholarship of teaching.

Setting New Standards

Anyone who has worked in interdisciplinary settings knows the enterprise is fraught with dangers. Rarely are we masters of more than one field. We do well to develop expertise in one discipline. Yet leadership in the music of the church demands that both theologian and musician participate in this collaborative, integrative work, and that they do so in the context of the congregation. For the music of liturgy to soar to its highest level, both musically and theologically, it must extract the best from the individual disciplines of music and theology. Further, for the music to have meaning for the liturgy, leaders must be convinced that the combination of the music and text create a meaningful union, that each is appropriate for the other. Finally, they also must be certain that the music and text are appropriate for the congregation's own praise and prayer. That is, the experience of the worshiper must be considered. Given the complexity of the enterprise, are we surprised that there are times when one of these necessary components is missing? Yet, and happily, this study provides nine examples of venues where this complex enterprise is functioning quite well, week after week, year after year.

Providing definitions for quality and excellence in these interdisciplinary, applied contexts is essential, because the standards for quality in the separate fields of theology and music do not always apply. The nine models of this book give us ideas about formulating these new definitions. First, quality in theology and music has to do with truth and honesty of expression. Good theology and good music are truthful in whatever form

they are expressed. Good, truthful music for worshi͜
simple or complex. A spiritual can be simple, beautiful,
cellent, just as a Bach cantata can be, and the spiritual ma͜
be the preferred choice for worship. Two writers are espec͜
articulate about what constitutes high-quality church mu͜ic.
They understand both the aesthetics of music and how music
functions in the liturgy.

Jane Marshall, a church musician, composer, and professor,
defines quality in worship music by (1) its universality, or its
ability to speak to all; (2) its timelessness, or its capacity to
be relevant across the years and for many generations; (3) its
ability to speak to the whole person, that is, body, mind, and
spirit, capturing not only the intellect but also the emotions,
and to garner a physical response; and (4) its capacity to speak
uniquely, in ways that transcend the ordinary.[5]

Frank Burch Brown, professor at Christian Theological Seminary, who writes succinctly about the intersection of religion and
art, says that a work can be judged for its aesthetic quality over a
period of time through comparative—and repeated—listening.
Regarding music used in worship, Brown would make the case
for clergy, congregation, and trained musicians to consider both
the aesthetic qualities of the music and the larger requirements
of worship. Further, he argues that the church needs art—including "classic" art—that challenges the congregation, art that
the Christian can grow into but not out of.[6]

High-quality music can be identified by those skilled and
trained in the craft of music, just as high-quality theology is
defined by standards in that field. Formal music training aims
to produce professionals skilled in constructing high-quality
music (composers), recognizing quality in music (those who
choose music), and translating that music into sound (performers). Granted, denominations do not have requirements
for their musicians, making the task of defining high-quality
church music a little more difficult. But music is a field of study,

just as theology is, and has its own standards of quality. A well-trained musician, like all the music leaders in our study, should be skilled in recognizing quality in music.

Different genres of music have their own standards for quality. Renaissance polyphonic choral music has criteria for excellence different from those for jazz. Time and distance give perspective to those with skill in a particular genre as they seek to refine the definitions of quality in a time and place. For example, those familiar with Western art music have developed some fairly predictable ways of determining quality in music, such as: Is the melody a good one? Does the piece of music have contour, using harmonic and melodic tension and release, building dynamically and musically to a climax and then subsiding? Does it make use of both variety and repetition? Is it musically coherent as a whole? Does the harmony flow naturally, and does the harmony adequately support the melody? Has the piece survived the test of time? These are a few questions one could ask about many pieces of music in the Western tradition, regardless of their complexity. Other genres require different questions.

Church music must meet an additional test: it must function well in worship. The music can be of high quality by other standards, but we need to ask if it is appropriate for the text and if it carries the theology of the liturgical moment well. Further, can the congregation sing it easily, so that worshipers can enter into the liturgical moment rather than being distracted by the music? Can they participate in the singing (when their singing is intended), are they relegated to the role of listeners by default, or must they work so hard to sing the words or the text that any sense of worship is lost? Does the music itself, even if the text is sacred, bring associations from a secular or other context that distract from the sacred intent?

The musicians in this study are constantly searching for the highest-quality music that carries the theology of worship for the day and then makes it accessible to the congregation, so that music becomes a vehicle for the praise and prayer of worship.

What about Style?

Much is written these days about style in church music, such as "contemporary style" or "praise-and-worship style" or "traditional style," but these terms are both hard to define and of much less importance than the matter of quality. If style is the point of departure for planning worship, planners can lose focus on the worship of God and emphasize the vehicle itself, pointing the congregation to the means instead of the object of worship. Then, as Frank Burch Brown would remind us, our tendency to advocate for our preferred style can lead us to the sin of pride. Choosing music based solely on style is like saying our mode of transportation is going to be a bicycle, so our destinations can be only those places where a bicycle will take us. Music history is replete with sacred music, much of it associated with the Christian church. We are fortunate to have many musical styles from which to draw for our worship, beginning with chant, which has always been associated with the church, and continuing to music composed by today's church musicians. To limit ourselves to any one style is to eliminate vast resources of theological wisdom and truth in worship. Conversely, for musicians to be able to choose from many genres and styles of music greatly enhances the possibility that worship will express deep theological truth for any time and place.

Eventually, a musical vehicle will have to be chosen to carry the worship for the day. If we use the "test of time" and "many listenings" criteria for quality, those styles that have been around longest will be the most reliable. In the Western tradition, for example, because classical music, folk music, and chant have stood the test of time, we can focus on how they might function in worship and how accessible they are for the congregation. Characteristics of these proven styles (memorable, singable music has a good melody, for example) can be used as standards for evaluating newer styles, but then further tests of function, accessibility, context, and appropriateness must be made. When the genres or styles used are less familiar to a congregation and its leaders, the standards within those genres or styles will then apply. (Note the musician at the cathedral on the West Coast, chapter 1, who contacted cathedrals in immigrant parishioners' countries of origin to identify the best music in their traditions.)

None of the churches in this study was chosen because of its focus on a particular style of music but rather because its music program has lasted. Yet these congregations use music from all periods of Christian worship history as well as music written recently, and some regularly commission new pieces. When different cultures come together for worship, that diversity broadens the music repertoire of worship. The congregation can serve as a catalyst to find the best music in the ethnic traditions of origin, and those styles then serve the liturgy and that congregation.

The number of available musical styles could be endless, but worship planners must consider whether each is appropriate, given the Scriptures for the day, the quality of the music itself, the theological truth to be conveyed, the meanings the musical style might suggest to the congregation, the ability of the congregation to sing in the style, and so forth. The point is that style is not to be viewed as an end in itself but rather as a vehicle that serves worship.

In the pages that follow are stories of people who have risen to this challenge of choosing the best music for worship and who purposely work beyond the confines of their training in theology or music to serve their congregations. They have put on the mantle of service, using their gifts and talents so that others can worship God in creative and meaningful ways. Gratitude and encouragement are qualities frequently displayed by these leaders.

I have only admiration and respect for the participants in this study and have learned more from them than they ever sought to teach. Their selflessness and gentle spirits, their superb skills in theology and music, their commitment to God and to the enabling of God's people for worship are offered for relatively small compensation. Yet they would be the first to say that this work is not about them but rather the work of the people. These are their stories, which they have given generously from their deeply held conviction that music is crucial to our understanding of God.

And the Heavens Opened

CHAPTER 1

Cathedral Music Transforms Parish and Community

THE CATHEDRAL IS IN A DETERIORATING NEIGHBORHOOD where poverty and homelessness in an otherwise thriving city had begun to affect the cathedral's ministry and its financial efficacy. The current music director came to the cathedral in the early 1980s, and the rector came a few years later. Together, they have moved the cathedral in a positive direction, both in its ability to provide leadership for the diocese and as a parish church that effectively serves its economically and ethnically diverse location. Both rector and musician believe that growth and change have occurred because the cathedral invested time and money in the arts. Part of the investment was a complete renovation of the interior of the worship space to form a place where the "full, active, and conscious participation of the people" was possible in liturgy. Part was equipping the music program with the personnel and instruments needed to lead the people. While the percentage of the budget given to the arts was initially greater than for other ministry areas, now the music and art budget, which has continued to grow, is a smaller percentage of the total budget. The growth of the parish congregation and the increase in resources from the generosity of the larger constituency the church serves have meant that a far greater percentage of the budget focuses on social needs.

The cathedral music program now includes nine cathedral choirs, choirs from outside the church that are invited to be in residence, instrumental ensembles, a choir school, and a variety of outside choral and instrumental groups that intersect with the liturgical music program in meaningful ways. All of this is accomplished with only three full-time professional musicians—a director of music, an organist, and an associate organist who also oversees the choir school. The rest of the music staff is part-time, including a music staff assistant, six paid soloists, and a variety of professional musicians in the metropolitan area who provide music on a fee-for-service basis. Included in this latter group are professional musicians who donate their services to the church and who in many cases are parishioners.

The comprehensive nature of the music program and the high quality of musical performance is not necessarily unique in the landscape of church music programs. Many cathedrals serve as models and inspiration for parish churches in their dioceses. What is unique and important about this music program is the integration of the music-making with a coherent and well-thought-out theology that establishes a foundation for catechesis—a means of teaching the faith—and focused outreach to the parish, the diocese, and the city. The mission of the church is always in the forefront of the music programming, providing a ministry that only the cathedral can offer, unequaled in other professional music venues in the city or in the parish churches that look to the cathedral for leadership.

Key to the program is the people who lead it, especially the priest and musician, both of whom have been in their positions for a significant portion of their ministries. Both have worked hard to achieve the mutual understanding of liturgy and music that is based on their shared commitments to their faith, their vocations, and a prayerful offering of their expertise in their ministry. The journey has not been without difficulty. But difficulty has been overcome by their respect for each other, openness, flexibility, and commitment to the larger vision. They have grown together in grace, and it is clear that the priest's leadership has been primary in the way the story has unfolded. His personhood is rooted in his calling and the serenity that results from his quiet confidence. The magnitude of the program and the difficulty that is bound to accompany the joy of "success" is mediated by a priest who knows what is truly important and by a musician who is unexcelled in his musicianship and dedication to both his craft and his faith.

Job Descriptions

Although the cathedral is large enough to operate as a business with a CEO at the helm, the person in charge identifies himself as "pastor." And the pastor sees his primary role as prayer leader. He believes that prayer is the "source and summit" of his task, and he sees music as integral to the prayer. He says, "If I care about the prayer, I care about the music. That doesn't mean that I 'meddle' in the music. I trust that [the music director] makes excellent musical judgments." Rather, he sees his role as a kind of cheerleader. Several times a year he may pop into a choir rehearsal on Sunday morning or Thursday night to tell the choir members what they mean to "this place." He believes there is no one who gives more volunteer time than the musicians. In his administrative capacity, every Monday morning he meets with the musicians to evaluate the weekend's liturgies and to plan for future liturgies. He sees it as his job to make sure the parts of the liturgy, the music, and the pastor's role all come together.

For the first ten years of the musician's tenure, he was in charge of only music. Then, during the next ten years, he served as both musician and liturgy director. After that job grew to be overwhelming, the roles were split. Nearly ten years ago, the cathedral assistant for liturgy became the director of liturgy, and the musician once again became responsible for only music. He plans and oversees anything relating to music in the cathedral. Because he is a musician first, this role often requires more administrative time than he would like. He works with cantors and psalmists, and prepares the schedules for the organists, for example. He complains mildly about "too much time at the desk." But he knows that administration is a necessary and important part of the larger picture and that it balances with the creative aspects of the job that he most enjoys.

He is also in charge of "environment," or how the visual and spatial experience affects liturgy, including such things as floral arrangements and banners. He explains, "People sometimes hear with their eyes, and if there is a disconnect between what one sees and hears, a tension is the result." In addition to being a member of the pastoral staff, he has community-building responsibilities, such as joint projects with non-Catholic religious groups. The rector often asks him for advice on projects involving design, whether that involves movement of furniture or people within the space for a liturgy or celebration, or more complex renovation or refurbishment. His aesthetic sense is trusted. He also has served on the board of directors of a national musicians' organization.

There is no music committee. The musician is responsible for choosing every acclamation, every hymn tune, the texts of the hymns, and who will sing them. The structure is hierarchical; he is responsible only to the pastor and the bishop.

EARLY MUSICAL FORMATION: SIMILAR EXPERIENCES

The priest grew up with training as a pianist. In high school, he took organ lessons with the organist at the cathedral, who was a graduate student at the time and who remains a parishioner today. When the priest went to Rome to study theology, he was an organist at the seminary he attended for two of his four years. He says he was never as good as he wanted to be, but he could "fake it" when necessary by improvising. He tells a story: when he was a pastor in a parish, the organist did not show up for a wedding at which he was presiding. He got another priest to say the mass. He played the processional, then came down from the organ loft to solemnize the vows, and went back up and played the rest of the mass. "So I sort of know what it means to be a church musician—it's part of who I am."

The musician grew up as the son of a conservative Baptist preacher, in a tradition where gospel music was the norm. He believes that experience helped inform him about what congregational singing could be, and not necessarily to accept what Catholics expected was possible for congregational song in the wake of Vatican II. While his dad was starting new churches, he began at age six to play either the piano or the pump organ for "Singspirations." He doesn't remember a time when music wasn't part of his life. He recalls at age four listening to a pianist who had played for tent revivals in the nineteenth century: "It was a lot more interesting than Dad's sermons." As a musician, he took the church music route, fully knowing that huge financial rewards were not ahead. But this was not a goal. Rather, "We get to do what we enjoy and get paid for it."

The musician enjoys working with non-musician parishioners such as lawyers, doctors, and custodians, enabling them to experience some of the joy they may not encounter in their daily work. He says, "Our greatest choir is the people who gather for the ten o'clock mass—not the choir itself, but rather the one thousand people who gather. They let me do a lot, and they come along for the ride." On Pentecost, four percussionists improvised everything from birds to wind machines, generating enthusiastic responses from those of the political left or right, the old or young, from symphony players to jazz band people—all knowing they had experienced something of the Holy Spirit as never before. A critical mass of parishioners carries the singing. Visitors often sit in back. Regular worshipers sit around the altar. During one of the site visits they sang "When I Survey the Wondrous Cross" to a psalm tone, and the musician conducted the hymn from the floor of the nave, putting in huge fermatas. The organ dropped out, and the people could hear themselves sing.

A VOCATION: THEOLOGIAN AS MUSICIAN, MUSICIAN AS THEOLOGIAN

The pastor's calling to the priestly ministry was largely due to people who were influential in his life as he grew up, including the organist who shaped his musical understanding. His family was "very Catholic" but not rigid in their faith. His father's first cousin, a venerable priest and the first native of the area to be ordained, baptized him and continued to mentor him through his college years. He and another family member who was a priest made the priesthood look attractive and real to the pastor. The pastor commented, "I think that God did speak to me through other people." He considers his calling "mediated" by the priests in his family, men who influenced his development as a young person.

He studied in Rome during the Second Vatican Council, a great moment in his life because so much change and ferment were in the air. "It was a privileged time to be there." He was ordained in Rome, and came back to the United States and took on roles as a pastor, mentor to seminarians, and administrator before becoming rector of the cathedral. The priest says he and the musician have learned each other's "hot buttons" and temperaments, and "all of the things that make us what we are. We've learned to appreciate each other and reverence each other's gifts."

The musician says he began the journey to being Catholic in junior high school, when he would sneak into a Catholic church, the original cathedral for the diocese, and fantasize about being an organist in that church. He enjoyed the immersion in sights, smells, and sounds, a gestalt encompassing the entire human experience. He worked in Baptist, Presbyterian, Danish Lutheran, and Episcopal churches before coming to the cathedral.

While he always took piano lessons, he thought that Chopin and the music he was playing on Sundays were not connected. He played the organ in a conservative Baptist church as a young person and was also asked to be the choir director. He studied English along with music as an undergraduate, and then attended a three-year graduate program in church music, studying with professors he describes as "extraordinary people." Later he received a Fulbright grant and went to Stuttgart, Germany, where he worked at a Catholic church and studied at the University of Tübingen. He has a DMA in conducting and two other degrees in music history.

It was the "extraordinary people" he encountered in his studies who helped form his theological understandings. One helped him understand music as an intellectual discipline as well as a performance skill. A conducting professor from a Mennonite tradition understood the centrality of music and prayer. Another had a passion for supporting amateurs making music and has been influential in the musician's choices about how the music program at the cathedral is structured. Another mentor was a Benedictine monk who urged him to consider moving from a post as music professor to the position at the cathedral, saying, "You and the cathedral need each other." It helped him understand the meaning of vocation. That is when he made the formal move to become Catholic. "The Church finally caught up with God and me."

Both priest's and musician's lives were changed in critical developmental years and at important career points by influential people with whom they were in conversation about their life choices.

Music, Space, and Liturgy: a Sacramental Union

The priest spoke of the "sacramental role of the aesthetic" as a sign of the unseen reality. "Music lifts hearts and spirits, provides beauty, and gives us a glimpse of glory. If the text is beautiful, it stretches us. At times a simple hymn or a glorious motet gives a glimpse of what is to come. These moments are not so uncommon."

He also spoke of music as a unifying force, a means of bringing people together. The belief in music-making as an important communal act influenced the renovation of the cathedral, which had very dry acoustics. The archbishop and the rector decided that the cathedral's acoustics were a liturgical issue, not merely an aesthetic one, important though aesthetics might be. The musician says, "The people of God needed their own instrument, a sonic space where they could hear themselves, space that would enhance what they do in the way that the body of a violin does. While our acoustic changes were very expensive, they have transformed how we sing." The space now lends itself beautifully to music and liturgy. At the same time, the visual aesthetics were considered, and the result of the renovation is both grandeur—sweeping open spaces from north to south and transepts from east to west—and intimacy: a central altar positioned so that no spot in the cathedral is far from it. A new organ was placed at the opposite end of the nave from the original organ (both playable from one console), so that the congregation is supported in its singing from both ends of the cathedral, another strategic decision in enabling the song of the people.

The space also has contributed significantly to the growth of the parish. The priest says that since the renovation,

> the size of the parish has tripled and has become a more "intentional" community. When you gather in a circle around the altar, you can sense the community. The music and the space reflect the kind of community we are, the way the people pray, and the way they connect to the liturgy.

The musician speaks of the unity of music and liturgy:

> In the Catholic Church there is no way to separate music from the liturgy. If there is only spoken text at mass, it does not come close to the fullness of what the Catholic liturgy is. It has been clear since 1967 that it is the liturgical dialogues that are the primary place for the congregation to sing. I believe

that the reason our congregation is a *great* singing congregation is that for well over two decades, we have sung those tiny little dialogues in which the church invites us to break down "you and me" and become "we."

And he points out that now, decades later, both the new *General Instruction to the Roman Missal* and the recent instruction from the American bishops, *Sing to the Lord*, define these little dialogues as the most important thing to be sung. In the renovated space, the congregation members get to hear themselves as singers. So the *place* where music is made cannot be separated from the liturgy; it is part of how the people pray. For him, the moments when he is moved to tears are not "at the brilliant performance of a Mozart piece" but rather when he hears "how incredibly these people sing."

Good Leadership Is Servant Leadership

The priest is clear about the kind of leader he intends to be and the kind of leadership he seeks in others. The musician both admires and tries to emulate that style of leadership. The priest says:

> A leader has to be able to listen and take the pulse of those he is asked to lead. A leader has to have clear vision. You have to be courageous at times, and sometimes make hard calls. You have to listen, and you have to learn. You have to be willing to go back and admit when you are wrong. Acknowledge failings. Appreciate people's gifts, and let them know that you appreciate them. You mustn't patronize them. In the church, a good leader is a person of prayer. It starts there.

He believes in collaborating and affirming, and, if necessary, apologizing.

The musician endorses the leadership of his priest:

My pastor is a good leader. He is "human." He has to deal with flaws in himself and in all of us. He makes mistakes, because he is willing to try new ways of doing things. He is continually pursuing the holy. I think a great leader is not one who hits the bull's-eye every time, but every time, he tries to hit the bull's-eye.

The musician hopes he can do that with the choir, even though he knows that he fails over and over. His enthusiasm and ways of explaining how the piece fits into the liturgy are the catechesis for the people he works with. He continues to look to the priest to see how that can be done. It can be tricky to navigate keeping the program on course and negotiating the human relations. "A good leader knows when to draw lines in the sand, or when not to. It is important not to draw the lines too quickly or too closely. When that happens, there is no way to work toward the commonly held values." He remembers the advice: "If you're going to say 'this is it,' be sure to wait forty-eight hours before telling anyone else that."

On Professional Musicians

Both priest and musician think of music as a professional endeavor in the church. Quality of musicianship is a matter of integrity for both those working within the cathedral and those on the outside looking in. The pastoral aspect of the music is the additional criterion that gives the music its meaning for the liturgy.

The priest believes that the professional musician "who has really earned his or her stripes—has the background, the certification, the education—is important to the life of the church." The musician should have musical expertise and knowledge of the church and its traditions, and bring that expertise and knowledge to bear in a way that "is sensitive to where the parish is at the moment, and where it wants to go." But he believes that the balance of the pastoral with the musical is equally important: "Probably the worst thing is for the musician to say 'I know what it should be' without reference to any other part of the operation. In the church, the musician is a pastoral minister, just as the others are. All have to respect each other."

He wants the musician to be respected as a musical professional, just as the pastor, theologian, religious educator, and social worker are professionals. The parish is a blending of professions and disciplines; a pastoral team is the goal. What the musician does affects religious education, for example. The cathedral has many outreach ministries, including a shelter for the homeless and a program of teaching English as a Second Language. Music is part of outreach and must complement the other forms of outreach.

The musician acknowledges the difficulty of being a professional musician who works primarily with amateurs in a music program. He comments:

> You never compromise musical standards but rather define carefully what those musical standards are: they need to be the "ear and the heart" of the assembly, and always truthful to the music that is chosen. That ideal manifests itself in a number of ways. For example, the music might be less difficult than would be chosen for professional performance venues. Yet when choir walks through the door on Sunday morning or at Thursday night rehearsals, they know they will be held to a pretty high standard—one that is professional.

On the other hand, he will not embarrass lay musicians by having them fail. If music seems too difficult, he will make a change. He always makes certain they understand what they will be doing for a Sunday liturgy. He adds:

> Except, perhaps, on Corpus Christi Sunday, when the liturgy will be catholic and Catholic—a street fair combined with awe-filled liturgical and theological moments all jammed together. The procession shows how being Catholic is the fullness of the human condition. It may seem cacophonous, but it won't be, because at the center of the celebration is the Eucharist.

The musician respects that the choir members are primarily volunteers and that he is there to facilitate their ministry. During a ten-month period, they spend the equivalent of five forty-hour weeks at the cathedral making music. Some drive an hour and a half for rehearsals and liturgies. This time spent in choir is a vital part of their spiritual growth. Early on, he established a chaplain of the choir who leads prayer, and the people take their needs to him. He sees the choir as a faith community.

The Music Program

The music program is funded through a combination of budgeted amounts, special gifts and fundraising efforts, and income from special events. The youth music program budget of $20,000 generates the income that it costs, so it is self-sufficient. Another budget item of $80,000 for special events, including sacred music concerts, organ concerts, and other seasonal events, is covered by income from tickets and donations.

A fairly elaborate mailing is sent out once a year detailing the music program and asking for donations to support it. The music and liturgy budget includes cantors' fees, honoraria for brass players, purchase of music, and the maintenance of organs, pianos, bells, and vestments. Twenty-five years ago music was 20 percent of the budget, and it is much less now, although the number of masses and soloists is the same. The music program directly generates $130,000 to $150,000 in revenue a year. In addition, a million-dollar capital fund paid for the new organ. For a choir trip to Rome, $700,000 was raised. None of the trip funds came out of parish funds.

ABOUT THE MUSIC

Perhaps one of the ironic pieces of this story is that in a cathedral steeped in the practice of music based on the ideals of Vatican II, very little of the music used has been written since the council.

The hymnal *Worship*, by GIA Publications, is in the pew rack; it is one of the more broadly based of the Catholic compilations available, drawing on the best of historical and even Protestant sources. Rather, the musician's own varied religious experience, rich educational background, European education, natural curiosity and creativity, and undoubtedly the theological and musical grounding of the priest allow choices of music from the best of past and present resources. Their own vision for creating a liturgy carried by "those little dialogues" with the people along with the Scriptures for the day give them the foundations for choosing music. Unaccompanied chant is used with ease, and at times even Latin serves as a unifying language among the many ethnic peoples the parish serves. No attempt is made to "attract" worshipers by using religious popular music of the day. Rather, the best quality music is made accessible to all for participation, chosen carefully with wisdom about what the congregants can sing, and how to help them sing it.

The Same Liturgy Draws Different Pieties

The cathedral uses the same liturgy throughout any one weekend despite the many different ethnicities and generations it serves. The leaders focus on the season of the church year and the liturgical implications of that particular day in designing liturgies. The priest acknowledges:

> Sunday evening feels the least like a community. There are young adults who don't register their attendance as part of the parish. The congregation at ten o'clock on Sunday is the most engaged. Participation is visible. The closer you get to the altar, the more the people are singing, and participating. The basic structure of the music is the same at all of the masses. If you're really tapping into the season and the liturgy, you're going to land pretty much at the same place for all the people at any one liturgy.

He believes the reliability, authenticity, and quality of the music are important to outreach: "Music attracts people here, and keeps them coming back, not just for performances, but for the liturgy." The music must be consistently excellent whenever it is offered in the cathedral.

UNIQUE TRADITIONS AT THE CATHEDRAL

Several unique traditions surfaced in exploration of the various liturgies offered at the cathedral. For example, there is a post-communion hymn of praise rather than a closing hymn at the end of mass. At the 5:30 p.m. weekday mass, a seasonal antiphon, such as the *Salve Regina*, is sung with no accompaniment. It is a simple but touching offering and an effective way to end the day.

On Good Friday, three hours of music and great preaching are added to the primary liturgy. Music such as Haydn's *Seven Last Words* or Pergolesi's *Stabat Mater* is offered in the context for which it was written and punctuated with preaching and prayer.

The cathedral has taken seriously its role as transmitter of the sacred treasures of Christian heritage, both liturgical and artistic, and as model, inspiration, and resource for parish churches. The musician says:

> Because Vatican II was mainly directed toward parishes, many cathedral programs went into eclipse. There was no real place for them in this liturgy, and they were uncertain of their new role. Long traditions are very rare in cathedrals in the United States. We have a few things: *The Christus Factus Est* canticle is sung all through Holy Week at various services, as it has been sung since the 1930s. The biggest tradition is the great organ in the back, which almost was torn out. It sounds the way it sounded one hundred years ago, when it was dedicated.

It creates a continuity of sound in the room and helps us all understand where we've come from.

The musician goes on to describe other traditions, such as using the same brass arrangement of "Jesus Christ Is Risen Today" that worshipers have heard at Easter for twenty-five years. Another sense of "home" is created at Christmas midnight mass, when worshipers hear the same extended timpani, trumpet, and organ introduction. On Pentecost they have come to expect something unusual—for example, one hundred flute players placed around the church, playing tones that evoke the mystery of Pentecost. The musician received complaints when a traditional Mozart work was used instead!

Another tradition begun by the current musician and rector is the inclusion of liturgical practices familiar to parishioners from varied ethnic backgrounds. The musician has telephoned his colleagues at the cathedrals in worshipers' countries of origin, such as Mexico, Brazil, the Philippines, and Indonesia, to learn how various traditions were expressed in the liturgies there. From that information, he was able to incorporate those traditions meaningfully and appropriately into worship at the cathedral. For example, a Filipino wedding tradition, a blessing of the wedding coins, or *arras*, was included in a wedding of a Caucasian and a Filipino during the weekend of one of the site visits. The bride and groom exchanged thirteen coins, each representing one of the thirteen universal tenets of marriage: love, trust, commitment, respect, joy, happiness, harmony, wisdom, unity, nurturing, caring, cooperation, and peace. The ritual traditionally served as a reminder of the groom's promise to fulfill his role as provider. Today, it is looked upon as a symbol of the security, mutual commitment, success, and prosperity in the couple's new life together. At the same wedding, "Manila Cathedral Alleluia" by Jesuit composer Eduardo Hontiveros was sung surrounding the Gospel reading.

OUTSIDE MUSIC GROUPS

Vatican II said the cathedral is obligated to preserve the great treasure of sacred music, as well as to foster new music-making. In that spirit, the resident choir program was started to encourage local community choirs and semi-professional choirs to sing music from the Catholic tradition. Local groups are invited to apply to become resident ensembles that perform concerts at the cathedral throughout the year. These ensembles are also available to sing liturgies, and because participants are professional singers and become acquainted with the religious traditions at the cathedral, they often augment the services of the volunteer choirs. The application process begins in January, and the season begins in September. There were four ensembles in residence the year of the study.

Some resident ensembles use the cathedral for rehearsal space, and some make recordings in the cathedral. In exchange, they lead the music for the liturgies—there are between six hundred and seven hundred a year, a number that would be difficult for the cathedral to cover with its own professional and volunteer musicians. The ensembles also bring into this holy space people who wouldn't normally come to the cathedral. And they enable the cathedral to fulfill one of the directives of the Vatican II documents—preserving, advancing, and celebrating the heritage of the great treasury of sacred music that has accumulated over the past fifteen hundred years.

The guest choir program, less formal than the resident choir program, invites choirs to apply to sing at the cathedral, usually to support the congregation's singing at a 5:30 p.m. Saturday mass. These choirs may be traveling or local choirs. Out of fifty to seventy applications a year, thirty are accepted. The regular participation of cathedral, resident ensemble, and guest choirs allows implementation of the belief that a choir is the ideal way to lead communal song, because there are no boundaries between choir and congregation as there are between the congregation and a cantor with a microphone or a loud instrumental accompaniment. A goal of the cathedral is to have a choir for at least three masses each weekend.

WHEN DISAGREEMENTS COME

With a liturgy schedule as full and complex as that of the cathedral, difficulties will occur. The question is how to address them, so that emotion does not get in the way of solutions.

A successful technique the worship leaders have found is the "Monday Book," which resides in the sacristy. The priest, musician, sacristan, and liturgy director can all write in it. If one of them perceives that a problem has occurred over the weekend, he or she can write in it—but not until Monday. Very often, by Monday morning the emotion has diminished, so leaders can write about the situation objectively, or the matter has become inconsequential and does not need to be written about at all. By Monday afternoon's meeting, the group is ready to deal calmly with whatever happened. Referring to a hymn text, the music director says, "Where true love and charity exist, God is always there."

Vatican II in Full Blossom

It is hard to imagine a place where music plays a more integral role in the liturgy and where the full, active, and conscious participation of the people in liturgy is more evident. The priest was trained in the midst of the Vatican II reforms. The cathedral was renovated to put these reforms into practice. The musician and the priest have worked and grown together as they have thoughtfully and prayerfully implemented the reforms week after week, year after year, in a setting of economic and racial diversity that would, under most circumstances, defy success. Yet the cathedral has grown not only in its reputation for the finest of music, but in its ability to aid the prayer of its people, no matter their ethnic origins, and to serve the needs of the poor as well—reflecting the flowering of Vatican II ideals, indeed.

A New and Living Way

CHAPTER 2

The Organ Anchors the Liturgy for a School and Church Community

By Annette Conklin

THIS THRIVING ROMAN CATHOLIC PARISH IN A MIDWESTern suburb had its beginning in 1946 with a few committed families holding services in a parishioner's home, then in a public-school building, and finally in the basement of its new school. This church building, dedicated in 1971, is located in a lake area of modest to substantial homes. The sanctuary is part of a complex that includes a eucharistic chapel, an education center, a large office area, and a school for kindergarten through grade eight.

The congregation numbers slightly more than fifteen hundred households, comprising a wide age group. Many of the older parishioners who were founding members are still active. New families continue to move into the parish, largely because of the school. Despite the public perception of the area as prosperous, there is a broad economic and educational range among the parishioners—people with advanced degrees as well as business people, some of whom are successful self-starters in private and personal businesses, and others who work with large corporations.

First Impressions

I arrived at the 10:00 a.m. mass on the first Sunday in Advent and entered the sanctuary, which seats about nine hundred people. With its soaring cathedral ceiling, the worship space is magnificent. It is built of poured concrete and warm woods, including massive red oak ceiling beams. The shape of the space resembles a concert hall shell: the pews fan out around the altar, and there are enough curves and angles to create an acoustically resonant sound. To the right of the altar are a grand piano and an organ, with pipes framing an immense modern stained-glass window in shades of red, orange, purple, blue, and yellow.

A greeter handed me a worship aid displaying a black woodcut of a man in robe and sandals holding a door ajar (representing the beginning of a new liturgical season?). It included information about the season of Advent and page numbers and titles of hymns for each part of the liturgy. As I looked for a place to sit, I noticed well-dressed people of all ages, including many families with children.

Before mass began, the male cantor rehearsed the piece to be sung during the preparation of gifts, and he called for "women only" to rehearse one verse and "men only" another. Despite the introduction of new music for the season, members of the congregation seemed actively involved in singing, opening their hymnbooks and following the hymns and responses. The music director sat at the piano; he and a young man at the organ often played the accompaniments together.

At the Sunday 5:00 p.m. mass, fewer people were in attendance, some arriving late and dressed more casually, many in jeans. In addition to organ and piano, a group of teen instrumentalists accompanied the singing and took some well-played solo turns. I noted that during the preparation of the altar and gifts, they sang a different song than at the earlier mass. This one had a catchier beat.

The Leaders

The pastor inherited a well-developed music program when he arrived three years ago. The music director, who has been here for twenty-eight years, is the person responsible for building the program. Each of them is well trained in his field, and both have a real commitment to high-quality worship and music in this parish.

FORMATION OF PRIEST AND MUSICIAN

The priest grew up in Iowa, in a family that encouraged him in music. He played in bands in elementary and high schools, starting on clarinet in fourth grade and then moving on to saxophone and concert bass clarinet. He sang in his college choral group. He says that his vocation to the priesthood was purely the work of the Holy Spirit. Thoughts of priesthood "were just there" when he was a senior in his Catholic high school, but he wrestled with his vocation for many years before accepting it.

After college, he entered the seminary, and received his Master of Divinity degree before ordination. Furthermore, he holds master's degrees in spirituality and counseling psychology and is a licensed chemical-dependency counselor. He also holds a doctorate in transpersonal psychology. For eleven years, he taught psychology and pastoral theology at a local Catholic university. He also is on the faculty of a summer liturgical music conference.

The musician's family home is in South Dakota. Though raised in a strong Catholic family, he never attended a Catholic educational institution. His early music education was in popular and folk genres, his first instrument being the accordion. He learned chording on the piano and on an electronic chord organ of the time. As an undergraduate, he majored in music education with an emphasis in vocal music. During his first year in college, he began his journey toward becoming a church musician. He became involved at the college's Newman Center and played guitar with a folk group, becoming its leader during his last three years of college.

His interest in church music was stoked when a chaplain at his college sent him to a workshop with the Rev. Lucien Deiss, the renowned French liturgist, Scripture scholar, and composer, who was involved in liturgical reform during Vatican II. The musician says it was at that workshop that he learned what the liturgy was all about and what the eucharistic prayer was intended to do. He says it was a "mind-body" experience, a strong formation that changed the way he did everything.

After graduation from college, he headed south to a university with a renowned music program, where he studied for a year with an organist who has trained many musicians who hold leading church positions today. "He [the organist and teacher] connected me to my spirit and helped me to see the beauty of the pipe organ. I practiced more that year than I had during my four years of piano in college," he said. He returned to the Midwest and later enrolled at a state university, where he earned a Master of Music degree in church music. It was a performance degree—voice, organ, and choral music—but no theology.

Defining Their Work

The priest oversees every element of parish life in this large, highly structured parish: administration, the school, pastoral ministry, faith formation, and worship and music. While maintaining overall responsibility in these areas, he gladly delegates to those who have expertise in each of them. He feels a strong responsibility to see that the liturgical life of the parish is being nurtured.

The musician's official title is director of worship and music. For most of his tenure here, he was director of liturgical music, while a pastor or a deacon oversaw the planning of the liturgy. Under this new pastor, his role has been expanded to include making liturgical decisions so that music and liturgy cohere. His primary duties are as choirmaster, cantor, organist, and director of the Alleluia Choir (grades four through eight). He oversees four part-time assistants and nine volunteer assistants. He also mentors the teenage organist, who has been an American Guild of Organists competition winner. He is the liturgical music resource person for the school. Either he or his part-time assistant plays for and prepares the school children for their weekly liturgy.

He has composed some liturgical music. Drawing on connections with church music publishers, and as a result of his position on the archdiocesan worship board, he has arranged composers' forums and a drum workshop for local church choir directors. During the summer he leads workshops throughout the United States. To sustain this busy life, he finds nourishment in his family, as well as in nature—enjoying quiet, streams, rocks.

VIEWS OF LEADERSHIP

The priest's concept of a good leader is "one who has an astute awareness of the community—one who delegates and builds community relationships and calls forth the gifts of the community."

The musician recalls a workshop in Milwaukee where the Rev. Alan Pyle spoke of "a leader who serves, a servant who leads," an idea that has always stuck with him. He notes, "As a choral conductor, you're the leader. You're the dictator. You're in an 'in-charge' position. And yet you are a servant of the liturgy. It's not about me. It's not about my music or the music I compose. It's about the assembly."

He sees the job of music director as being musical, liturgical, and pastoral: liturgical in the sense of understanding the ebb and flow—what's important; pastoral in the sense of choosing the text that is put into the mouths of the congregation Sunday after Sunday. He believes that one of his most important tasks is the spiritual formation of what he considers his largest choir—the congregation.

He adds, "You really have to work at your own spiritual life. Take time to pray, and attend to your spirituality." It's hard. It's essential. It's always a struggle."

PLANNING AND EVALUATING LITURGIES

Both priest and musician believe that music and liturgy need to be deeply rooted in Scripture. For the Sunday Eucharist, they work from the lectionary. The musician consults with the pastor on which rituals they are going to use—"Shall we do a sprinkling rite? An anointing mass?"—and then uses resources that are linked to the Scriptures for the day to complete the task. He is very happy with the hymnal *Gather Comprehensive*, second edition. He also uses Liturgy Training Publications (LTP) resources; Liturgical Press materials from St. John's Abbey, Collegeville, Minnesota, for background in liturgy; and *GIA Quarterly* magazine. He has on file all of the planning he has done for liturgies for the past three three-year cycles of the lectionary. In planning any given liturgy, he might pull out a file from last year or last season, review a liturgical structure or format that he found successful, and plug in whatever music he wants to use that weekend. He plans the choral music a year in advance during the summer months.

The music ministry schedule for each month is put up on the parish website. In addition to the music to be sung each weekend, it lists song leaders, organists, and choirs for each mass. A seasonal rehearsal and liturgy schedule is available online as well.

Priest and musician meet weekly to review the weekend masses as well as the Wednesday morning school mass. This evaluation includes the use of instruments: What do the parishioners and their instruments add to the prayer? Should there be more organ accompaniment and less piano, or vice versa? How about using timpani? They sometimes have short discussions between masses on Sunday. If, in their evaluation, the eucharistic ministers or the readers or ushers are not functioning well, they will meet with these individuals to find a solution. The musician says he thinks a pastoral musician or leader has to be flexible. "We need to be able to adjust, be calm and patient when sometimes things don't happen the way we planned them."

The priest says he believes that having a music director who is a trained professional is a "gift to the community" and notes that after working with someone on that level, he has become somewhat spoiled. He believes that it is essential for a pastor to have a strong relationship with the music minister. In fact, he is convinced that the community will notice, if only on a subliminal level, if the two of them are not on the same page.

INVOLVEMENT OF THE LAITY

A lay worship and music advisory committee was formed in 2001 to help implement the plans made by priest and musician. Members feel free to propose ideas of their own, too. The committee includes lectors, ushers, sacristans, choir members, eucharistic ministers, greeters, and servers—one person from each group. The committee members reflect upon the seasons of the year and are involved in scheduling and coordination. They have subcommittees, which include visual arts and sacred music and art events. The music director is the staff liaison on the committee. The pastor, who expresses strong appreciation for the group's work, attends the meetings on occasion.

Parish volunteers have helped create an environment that makes it possible for the congregation to worship the way it does. The music director notes, "They offer their time and talent for the various liturgical ministries—serving at the altar, reading Scripture, distributing Holy Communion, preparing materials before worship, rehearsing choral and instrumental music during the week and before liturgies. They have tended plants and candles, created fabrics and designs for the worship space inside and outside the building."

THEIR IDEAS ON WORSHIP

"Worship and music are the core and heartbeat of this faith community," states a ministry pamphlet published on the occasion of the parish's sixtieth anniversary. Priest and music director support wholeheartedly the Vatican II directive that the assembly be actively involved in the liturgy. And they believe that all members of the parish—from older "traditionalists" to teens and young adults who grew up post–Vatican II should worship together.

Music in Liturgy

The priest believes that the place of music in liturgy is to draw people to a deeper, richer, and fuller experience of prayer. He explains:

> We are all one body. The musical element is part of our prayer together. It touches our hearts and our souls. Music in liturgy needs to be deeply rooted in Scripture and to assist in spiritual awareness. It should not be entertaining. In fact, it enhances and enriches our prayer by not being entertaining. Someone needs to ask if some types of music assist us in experiencing the sacred better than others.
>
> People are hungry for mystery, and we've lost it. How do we regain a sense of reverence in the liturgy, and have it come from the inside rather than imposing it?

The priest has always loved Gregorian chant, and is pleased that during Lent the congregation sang some music a cappella and in Latin. He is happy that the student body in the school is learning to sing mass responses in Latin, because he sees this as a way to continue the traditional sacred music of the past.

The music director understands music as the fiber and the glue that hold the parts of the liturgy together. "Music is the servant of the liturgy. It helps the ebb and flow. Music moves quickly from the ear to the heart and soul . . . The tunes are important, but the texts that are selected are crucial."

All Ages Worshiping Together

Both priest and musician are committed to the idea that all ages should worship together, and they agree that this approach is always a challenge musically. The priest comments:

Those parishioners who were very young in the sixties might say, "Let's move on with the new. Why are we doing that old stuff? We're moving backwards in the church." On the other hand, the traditionalists might say, "There are songs that are important to us, and we don't sing them anymore." One of the greatest reasons I became a priest was my connection to the community of a parish of all ages—to pray with them and experience life's progression with them. I want it to be a community prayer, no matter what the liturgy. I think it's good for the young to pray with the traditional [pre–Vatican II] hymns and vice versa [for the traditionalists to experience contemporary music]. My goal at the 5:00 p.m. Sunday mass is not to isolate the teen participation there, but to have teens actively participate in the prayer of the entire community.

Likewise, the musician firmly believes that each service should be representative of the entire membership of the parish. He comments, "'People of God' is all ages, all colors, all preferences. To separate them out would be doing a disservice to the body of Christ."

So how does he accomplish this goal musically? The music is the same for all the masses, with the exception of the piece sung during the Preparation of Gifts. He "bends" the music toward contemporary or traditional by varying the accompanying instruments at the different masses.

The organ is used at every mass, although probably least at the Saturday 5:00 p.m. mass, which most often makes use of piano, flute, viola, saxophone, and drums. The Sunday 8:00 a.m. mass most often simply has a cantor and the organ. At 10:00 a.m.—the family mass—organ and piano are almost always used, and harp, flute, or handbells might be added, or occasionally guitar, violin, viola, and cello. The Sunday 5:00 p.m. mass uses more guitar and less organ, and usually there are two or three percussion instruments. Often there are viola and violin, and occasionally French horn and trombone.

Vatican II

Both pastor and music director thoroughly support the guidelines of Vatican II: that music forms an integral part of the solemn liturgy, and that the liturgy promotes the full, conscious, active participation of all the people.

The musician says that these are the two principles that he lives by and that shape his ministry:

> I wouldn't have stayed in this ministry without those guidelines. I implement [them] daily. I select music for the liturgy so that the people can actively participate. Of course, they can be participating in silence by listening, too. We had done that for centuries before Vatican II. Then we went in the other direction—everybody sang everything. We've hit a better balance now. If the liturgy is done well, music can be offered on behalf of the congregation. For instance, on Good Friday, when the choir sang "When I Survey the Wondrous Cross," they [the assembly] weren't singing, but I knew they were there.

The pastor believes that the changes wrought by Vatican II were undoubtedly needed. He would not advocate a return of pre–Vatican II pietistic practices, but he is concerned that the younger generations have lost knowledge of the church's history and the sense of reverence and mystery that was present in pre–Vatican II liturgy. He would like to regain this sense of reverence and mystery in today's liturgy.

Music in the Parish

The musician says that when parishioners travel, they often return feeling grateful for the quality of music and liturgy they experience in this parish. They have shown their appreciation by providing funds for high-quality instruments and hymnals.

And they and their children participate in the many choirs and instrumental groups that have been formed over the years.

Vocal Ensembles

After the new church was built in 1971, some singers and guitarists—later called the Glory and Praise Singers—got together and began rehearsing in homes. The group disbanded about ten years ago—its members are now busy traveling and being grandparents—though some of them still sing at the Saturday 5:00 p.m. mass, the one that a parishioner has described as "short, quick, and good."

From the beginning, the parish had a choir. The first paid choir director was hired in 1978. Under the current music director, the choir flourished. In November 1986 the choir combined with an area choral society to present Gabriel Faure's *Requiem*; directing the performance was a partial requirement for the music director's MM degree.

Today there are several choir groups: preparatory choirs that train children as young as three years old through fourth grade; a youth choir; the Sunday 5:00 p.m. musicians, known as "S5"; a men's chorus; the Sunday 10:00 a.m. choir; Schola, a funeral choir; and a handbell choir. The Sunday 10:00 a.m. singers, who are auditioned, rehearse on Thursday nights and sing challenging choral music of all styles and periods.

The musician puts a high priority on training the children. He wants them to be able to sing the Sanctus, the Hosanna, and the Greek Kyrie. The younger preparatory children's choirs sing for parish masses at least four times a year. The older choir (up to grade eight) may sing seven or eight times a year, including Christmas, Palm Sunday, or Holy Thursday.

The Organ Project

When the music director arrived at the church, it had a Baldwin electronic organ. In 1982, some fifteen years after Vatican II, when many Catholic parishes were moving away from the organ, he prompted the pastor and the parish council to begin a dedicated organ fund—a project that lasted twenty years. Over the years parishioners and friends made large and small contributions to the fund. They presented benefit concerts and sold greeting cards, bookmarks, tapes, CDs, and books to help pay for the organ.

After much discussion and a recommendation from the musician's former organ teacher and mentor, the organ design committee chose a nationally known pipe organ company to build the instrument. The installation was done in three phases: phase 1 was competed in January 1997, phase 2 in April 1999, and phase 3 in June 2002. The resulting organ has three manuals, thirty-four stops, and forty-one ranks.

The parish was involved in the installation in a hands-on way. Fifty or sixty volunteers, including seventh- and eighth-grade students, carried in materials over the three-phase span. There was a "pipe brigade" of people handing pipes along a line from the truck into the church.

The music director thinks that the involvement of volunteers was a strong reminder that it is a pipe organ for the people— young and old. "It had a great impact on these volunteers. They gained a greater understanding of the organ and much appreciation for the wood and metal craftsmanship. The congregation's appreciation grew as it was played for liturgies. The people were relieved and delighted at how it complemented the existing design of the church."

He believes that the sonority and range of an organ are essential for leadership. "It helps people sing. It is the glue of the liturgy. It can be used for the prelude, for expanding ritual music. It can touch people's hearts. There is no substitute for the sound from a wind-blown pipe, the natural vibrations in the air."

RESOURCES AND BUDGET

The parish owns a six-foot, nine-inch Kawai grand piano, purchased through ten donors in 1986. It also has timpani, congas, a variety of hand drums, electric bass guitar, mandolin, four octaves of handbells, and a bass viol that was a gift from a parishioner.

The musician is in charge of the budget of about $135,000, which includes salaries, benefits, the sound system, instrument maintenance, and office supplies. His two assistant choir directors are paid, and his student organist receives a small stipend, as does the children's choir coordinator.

He sees that the Choristers Guild magazine, *The Chorister*, is given to the directors of the children's choirs. He also encourages his directors and leaders of groups to go to National Association of Pastoral Musicians institutes, guitar schools, and other professional continuing education programs, with the parish paying part of the cost.

Keeping a Musical Balance

The musician works with a variety of styles of music. His hymnal of choice, *Gather Comprehensive,* second edition, includes contemporary and traditional hymns, folk-style and classical pieces, some of which are piano/guitar-based and others more organ-based.

He might also introduce African or Honduran tunes, music from the Taize Community, spirituals, and gospel music. In his opinion, spirituals are the most effective music for participation, sung a cappella. He likes early American hymn tunes and declares that anything that works with drums is also good for participation, citing as an example, "What Star Is This, with Beams So Bright." "It's a dance tune. You've got to have drums. And the voice can carry it."

He becomes passionate when discussing contemporary Christian radio music, which can be heard on at least four stations in town. He feels that Christian rock is a difficult style for communal, participatory song. According to him, many of the texts in that style do not fit the Catholic liturgy, and using just this music in the liturgy can turn it into "worship entertainment."

Occasionally someone will ask if a contemporary Christian tune heard on the radio could be sung during the preparation of gifts, and he bends and allows it, but he is becoming less and less open to it. "On the other hand," he observes, "You can't just cut it off. I know it's going to improve. There are going to be some good texts out there, so I'm going to keep looking."

A vocal minority in the parish does not like the blending of styles. At one time there were eight to twelve individuals on both ends of the spectrum (contemporary/pop and traditional) who wanted a mass each week in just their style. The music director says that these requests have lessened greatly since this pastor came. "His support and appreciation of the music ministry's [diverse] music selections has seemed to quiet these few."

The priest, in turn, gives the musician credit for trying to hold a balance between traditional and contemporary music. He cites the use of the pipe organ at every mass as one way the musician achieves that balance.

WHEN CONFLICT ARISES

One year, when planning a First Communion service, the priest and musician decided to have the children be seated with their parents and receive communion with their families. They wanted to avoid putting the children "on a pedestal" or showing them off. They found out that a teacher had already announced to the parents that the children would sit as a group in their own area, separate from their families, and that they would receive communion before anyone else. So priest and musician called a meeting with teacher and parents. They explained that the liturgy could flow better and be more family-oriented if the children sat with their families. They also proposed that the children gather around the altar on both sides of the priest during the Eucharistic Prayer and return to their families at the sign of peace. This would allow the children to have great visibility for the most important prayer and still be with family for the sign of peace and reception of communion. This plan was met with agreement.

The musician says that one of the great gifts of the pastor is that he's always helping to clarify. He himself has learned that when conflict arises, remaining calm and going to plan B or C is a necessary skill for a liturgical minister. He calls it "on the spot flexibility" or "improvisation on a theme."

Working Together

The liturgical and musical life in this parish is vibrant and strong. Pastor and music director appear to have a healthy working relationship. Each respects the gifts of the other. The musician appreciates the pastor's support of the music ministry and his ability to listen and clarify. The priest appreciates the musician's talent and professionalism, and thinks his ability to incorporate a wide variety of music into the liturgies is important in reaching the wide diversity of ages in the parish.

The congregation is actively involved in many aspects of the musical and liturgical life of the parish. Members serve on the worship advisory committee, participate in the many choirs, including those for very young children, and volunteer as musicians to play at the liturgies. They contributed funds for high-quality instruments and hymnals. They held benefit concerts and sold bookmarks, CDs, and books to raise money for the organ fund, and they carried the pipes and other materials to prepare for its final installation.

The organ has helped to keep the balance between traditional and contemporary music in the parish. Because it is used at all masses, it anchors the liturgy, providing constancy, while other musical aspects—the blending of musical styles and the variety of accompanying instruments—allow the parishioners to experience worship in a diverse and satisfying way.

Priest and musician continue to search for music that will deepen the prayer of the assembly while enabling worshipers to participate as one body in a joyful celebration of the liturgy.

Rest A While

CHAPTER 3

A Small Urban Catholic Parish Loves to Sing

By Annette Conklin

THIS SMALL CATHOLIC PARISH IN A LARGE MIDWESTERN city almost did not survive when, about thirty years ago, an interstate freeway was built within two blocks of the church, cutting up the neighborhood. But survive it did, largely because of the efforts of a former pastor who helped establish it as a "parish of choice," meaning that very few parishioners live nearby. Most choose to come because of the liturgy and music, the emphasis on social justice, and the quality of preaching.

The congregation numbers approximately three hundred households from fifty zip codes. For the most part, the parishioners are educated and intellectually sophisticated. Many hold advanced degrees, and several are professors at a nearby state university and a local Catholic university.

The nearly century-old building, a wooden two-story structure with twenty wide steps leading up to the entrance, is newly refurbished inside and out. Connected to the church proper is a fellowship hall for small gatherings and dinners. Adjacent to this is an area with office space for the parish administrators.

Three liturgies are offered each weekend—a Saturday evening mass at 5:00 p.m., and Sunday masses at 8:15 and 10:00 a.m. The most vibrant and well attended is the 10:00 a.m. choir mass.

First Impressions

I attended two 10:00 a.m. Sunday services at the parish. At the first visit, the priest greeted people warmly as they entered the small vestibule. Most of the social interaction was occurring within the nave, where there was much smiling and chatting. Everyone seemed to know everyone else. The interior of the church is small and intimate. A round, leaded stained-glass window above the altar area is balanced by a similar window at the entrance of the church. Five rows of pews are interrupted on the front left side of the worship space to allow space for a Yamaha grand piano and a few instruments. The small choir stands to the left of the lectern near the piano. The balcony in the rear of the church holds no organ. All age groups were represented, including many families, though I did not observe much racial diversity. Parishioners wore simple, comfortable clothing. The pianist was clearly in charge of the music. The small choir of fourteen was divided equally between men and women. In the absence of a printed order of worship, hymn numbers were posted on the wall and announced by the cantor. The choir sang no anthems but rather reinforced the music for the congregation. When the singing began, the church resounded with the voices of the assembly. People seemed to know the music well, and the pastor's fine baritone voice was evident.

My second visit was on Pentecost Sunday. As I entered the church, parishioners were again chatting in the pews. The music director welcomed everyone and announced the first hymn. In addition to the choir and the piano, there were two trumpets, a trombone, two horns, a clarinet, and two flutes. This musical group, composed mainly of youth, accompanied the singing throughout the mass. During the communion, the musicians played an instrumental arrangement of Bach's "Jesu, Joy of Man's Desiring." The lector was a teenager, and I recognized the cantor as a nationally known composer of Catholic congregational music.

There were three unusual aspects to the Pentecost liturgy: (1) During the first reading, from Acts, one parishioner after another stood and spoke quietly, each in a different language, until the church was filled with the murmuring of these dissonant voices—a bit of "theater" that was strikingly effective. (2) Instead of the spoken creed, the priest led the assembly in singing "Renewal of Baptismal Promises" by David Haas.

> *Cantor*: We do believe!
> *All*: We do believe! This is our faith,
> This is the faith of the Church.
> We are proud to profess it, in Christ Jesus. Amen!
> Amen!

(3) After communion, a short "lay reflection" was given by a member of the parish who said he worked in food service at a local hospital where fourteen languages are spoken. His topic was "Where Is the Church?" (I was told later that this was a "one-time event," and its purpose was to call attention to immigration issues.)

Because it was Pentecost Sunday, there was a printed outline of the liturgy, the page numbers of hymns to be sung, verses of the sequence for Pentecost, music for the psalm, responses, refrains, and the entire closing hymn. Most of the music could be found in the hymnal in the pew racks, *Gather Comprehensive,* second edition. The music director, sitting at the piano, conducted the instrumentalists, and a choir member raised his hand to bring in the assembly. Their voices again made the rafters ring.

The Leaders

The priest has been in the parish for five years, the music director for sixteen. This is the priest's first pastoral assignment. Because of teaching duties at a local seminary, he is at the parish only three to five hours a week, mainly for the Saturday evening and Sunday masses and other liturgies. The music director's position is part-time as well. A relatively large staff of six or seven people runs the parish during the week.

FORMATION OF THE PRIEST/PASTOR

The last two or three pastors not only could sing well but also were actively interested in promoting singing in the parish. When the previous pastor left after eleven years, he encouraged this priest to apply for the job.

One reason he may have been chosen is that he had been well trained as a musician. He was the oldest of six children growing up in a posh suburb. His parents did not have formal music training, though his father was an accomplished singer and all of the children were encouraged to play the piano or sing. He sang in a boys' choir in his Catholic grade school, where students received music lessons every day as part of the curriculum. The choir director who taught those music classes became a friend and mentor. He entered the priesthood late in life and, sadly, died at age fifty-eight, six weeks after being ordained. The choir director's influence led to the pastor's decision to join the priesthood.

This pastor continued his music involvement in his teens, singing in his high school's concert choir and serving as a cantor at various churches from age fifteen on. He sang in choir all four years in college as well. After college, he joined two semi-professional choirs—a Bach Society chorus and another chorale. He took voice lessons virtually all of his adult years, beginning with the wife of a Danish Lutheran pastor, the same woman who had taught his priest-mentor. After his seminary training and during graduate school at a Jesuit school of theology, he enrolled at a school of music as a non-degree student, studying with a wonderful vocal teacher who was in her mid-nineties. He sang in some of the school's ensembles—"a lot of opera and nineteenth-century German music." He earned two advanced degrees in sacred theology.

Before entering the seminary, he'd had a strong preference for traditional church music—English anthems and standard hymnody as well as organ music. At the seminary he worked with a musician he refers to as a "great experimenter." She directed the choir, taught music classes, and coordinated the cantors. He says he learned from her that "there is no such thing as liturgy that is not musical." But she was convinced that a congregation couldn't possibly do traditional music and be "a Vatican II parish." The pastor now says, "I think she was wrong." But it was at the seminary that he learned to appreciate all types of liturgical music, especially music written after Vatican II.

FORMATION OF THE MUSICIAN

The music director, a woman in her late forties, started at the parish as a substitute pianist and has directed the music for the past fifteen years. Her family was a musical one. As a child, she watched her parents sing in their parish choir. She loved choral music and often sang three-part harmony with her sisters. Piano was her instrument from second grade through college and beyond. She recalls that sometimes it seemed as if she were the only pianist in her high school, and she was often pulled out of classes to accompany groups. Her college degree was in music education, with piano as her major instrument. She also took voice lessons and sang in a mixed-voice chorale. After graduation, she found no music positions available and so did substitute teaching in the schools; that experience, she says, "just about did me in." She also did substituting for church positions, but it never occurred to her to be a church musician. She substituted at this church for six months before being offered the position of music director.

DESCRIPTION OF THEIR WORK

The priest's main job is to preside and preach at three weekend masses and at other liturgies such as weddings and funerals. He also serves on the parish's liturgy committee. He teaches systematic theology in the school of divinity of a nearby seminary and also in the graduate lay program at the adjoining Catholic university. He also does some teaching in the summers at another university's school of theology, and he gives workshops in parishes throughout the archdiocese. The parishioners appreciate his well-prepared homilies, which can be accessed on the parish's website. He says that, by his choice, he has virtually no input into music decisions, although the music director would be open to his suggestions.

The musician directs the adult choir and accompanies the three weekend masses, weddings, and funerals, a job she estimates to require about thirty hours a week. She says she has never called in sick, nor has she ever signed a contract. When there is no song leader, she leads the singing from the piano. At the 8:15 a.m. Sunday mass, she serves as cantor about half of the time.

Although she often both serves as musician and prepares the liturgical content for each service, she does not want to be called a liturgist. But over the years, she has attended many weeklong summer workshops at the liturgical music conference where the pastor teaches. She also has attended many archdiocesan workshops and meetings offered by the archdiocese on the General Instruction on the Roman Missal. Her theological training may be informal, but it informs her work in substantive ways.

She does a lot of arranging of music for the choir, and has mastered the *Finale* software program for music notation. Though some hymns are written in parts in the hymnal, she sometimes adds other voices to accommodate the abilities of the singers in the choir. To facilitate singing for the congregation, she says, "If it goes above a D, I transpose it." She wants the singers to know they can sing the range of the pitches and to be familiar with the tunes: "They *have* to be comfortable. The community is the choir, and the choir augments the community."

She finds nourishment in going to concerts, including some at a nearby Lutheran college known for its highly rated music program, where her daughter is a student and where she sometimes hears a piece she might choose to use with the choir. She seems greatly stimulated by her job. In her words:

> I just love it. I never get sick of it. It's always changing. I always have the drive to create and be part of the experience for the congregation at a liturgy. There's no bigger high. I tell the choir, "This is a goose-bump moment." You always try to go for the goose-bump moment.

But she says she can get a bit burned out and always enjoys the summer break with no choir. Sometimes she will go to another parish to experience music from the pew. Parishioners who have visited another parish during the summer will often tell her, "You can't believe how bad it is out there." She says that after fifteen years she still gets comments from parishioners who have been moved by a particular piece of music, and say, "That was incredible."

A parishioner who is not a member of the choir but is involved in a music profession volunteered to me, "She is outstanding." The pastor himself described her as "a treasure to this place."

VIEWS OF MUSIC IN LITURGY

The musician and the pastor both see the importance of music in liturgy and value the integrity with which it must be chosen and implemented. In the words of the musician:

> The best choices of music convey the deeper meanings of the Scriptures or use the actual words from Scripture in the text. If the music selected has a melody of good quality and is executed professionally (not necessarily by professionals) and is chosen to reflect the sacred Scriptures read at mass, the people will come to respect and appreciate the music ministry in their parish.

She continues:

> Music should bring people into deeper prayer and not distract
> from prayer. It should inspire and make people want to par-
> ticipate. The music ministers here are expected to put in time
> training and rehearsing the music each week. They realize the
> responsibility they have been given in leading their congrega-
> tion in sung prayer. The assembly senses, maybe unconsciously,
> that this is not a performance they are attending, but a coming
> together in worship and song for the glory of God.

In the words of the pastor:

> Good worship must involve everybody doing his or her part.
> When we get questionable musical outcomes in liturgy,
> people talk about it. We've seen what's possible when people
> really care and are willing to expend themselves [to create] a
> high-quality worship experience. This makes for an exception-
> ally positive atmosphere in church.

Both understand that effort is required to prepare music for
liturgy, and that expectations must be placed upon the people
to ensure that it is offered well. When that happens, genuine
worship results.

Concept of a Good Leader

The pastor describes a good leader as "one who empowers
others." He thinks this leadership characteristic is part tem-
perament and part theology. He explains, "I have no trouble
being an overseer. But people who are well trained in their
fields should be honored for what they know. We couldn't
survive if people didn't step up to the plate." Asked how the
congregation enables him to lead, he responded: "They trust
me, and they are affirming of my leadership. Our culture is

not fundamentally pastor-driven in the sense of people relying upon me to initiate new projects or to be the primary support for various ministries."

The idea that a good leader empowers others is shared by the music director. She believes that an effective leader facilitates the good qualities in another person—"draws out their strong qualities and lets them fly with it." She tries to do that with the musicians she leads. But sometimes being a good leader means you must remove roadblocks for others. She once encountered a cantor who simply could not do the job—who couldn't learn her part even after listening to tapes. So she had to fire the woman—a difficult task, but, she explains, "You have to respect the people's prayer, too. If something is distracting their prayer, you can't let that go on."

Speaking of cantors, she says, "You can't lead unless you know it well yourself. You don't come and wing it—*ever*." She has "spies" in the congregation to find potential cantors, and those approached usually feel honored to be asked. Though cantors are not paid, she trains them, usually one-on-one. She learned something after dismissing that one cantor—the cantors have to be able to read music. Now she doesn't offer anyone the job without an audition. "It's harder to un-invite them than to invite them, so you must be very careful."

Planning the Liturgies

The priest plays no role in planning the music. He relies on and respects the music director's decisions. Usually there is a real integration between the homily, the Scriptures, and the music. Often he is amazed that this happens, since the integration is not the product of a lot of planning.

> The music director may ask, "Should we sing the eucharistic prayer? Do you want to do the acclamations during Lent?" And that's about it. I never initiate. I don't have to. She has

excellent judgment. She's well trained in music and liturgy. She knows what she's doing. Why interfere with that? We almost never do music that I am unhappy with here.

The musician echoes this observation. People think she coordinates with the pastor, "but the truth is, we don't. The pastor is preaching on the lectionary readings. If the music is reflecting the readings, you don't need to talk to the priest, because you're both focusing on the same thing."

Her method of preparing the music is to study the readings every single week, to put them into her own words, and then to match the music to the readings. She has done a synopsis of all the readings for all three cycles in the Lectionary. Each week, she types up a sheet with a list of the music to be sung and distributes it to the pastor and the singers. The cantors get the music list in the mail a week ahead. The choir members have it on their chairs at rehearsal on Tuesday. On the weekend, she places the sheet where the pastor is getting vested for mass. She says very simply, "It works."

Honoring the Guidelines of Vatican II

The pastor says he takes the Vatican Council at its word:

We honor the call of Second Vatican Council that the gathered community be formed, supported, and empowered in their "full, active, and conscious participation" in the liturgy. This value is primary above all others in regard to our liturgical life here. If there are options to sing or not to sing, we sing. The choir is very good. They have the wonderful ability to be the choir and yet to be of service. Worship is a holistic event, not just words. It has to engage the whole body. If it is good news we're talking about, it has to involve the expression of such. It is a communal act—it brings people together. That has been a tradition at this parish forever.

But he believes the culture of the Catholic Church is changing. Liturgical musical experimentation peaked after Vatican II, and now such experimentation does not seem as welcome in his diocese. He very much admires the religious order of monks at his alma mater, their interest in the arts, their theological integrity, and their primary concern for the liturgy, which he sees as "a culture that is open to legitimate exploration." He wishes that this exploration could continue.

The music director says that "full and active participation by the people" is her favorite phrase from the Vatican II documents:

> It is the people who are doing the liturgy—not the choir or the priest doing it for them. We're all doing it together. I think that's what Vatican II was trying to get across to us. I think they get it here—by osmosis. Full and active participation by the people is my whole mission, right here.

However, whereas the Vatican II documents cite the primacy of the organ, the pastor stated that there is not the slightest interest in having an organ in this church, and the music director agrees. The parish had one, but no one liked the sound, so it was donated to a convent. No one misses it. Everyone loves the piano.

The Music Program

The parish does not put a lot of money into the music program. Only the music director is paid, and she is part-time. All of the cantors and choir members are volunteers, as are most of the ad hoc musicians who help out from time to time. On a few of the high holy days, the parish hires some professional string players.

Resources and Budget

The parish owns one African drum, two octaves of handbells, a Yamaha grand piano, and an old upright piano in the rehearsal room. When a parishioner heard that the parish needed a new piano, he donated $10,000 toward it. After the musician found a good-quality used grand piano at a sale at a nearby university, the finance committee made an announcement asking if anyone else would donate toward it. The music director was amazed. "People were standing in line with checks—$1,000, $500." The parish raised enough to purchase the piano, a piano cover, and a piano light, and there was still money left over.

The modest music budget covers piano tuning, repair and maintenance of the two pianos, a subscription to the *GIA Quarterly*, new choral music, copyright license, and appreciation gifts for the music ministers at Christmas. The music minister's salary does not come out of the music budget, but the pastor says that she would be among the highest paid if, instead of receiving a flat stipend, she were paid by the hour.

For the seven years under its first music director, the reconstituted parish had no choir. The people took ownership of the liturgy, including congregational singing. When the next music director started a choir, she met much resistance, because the assembly thought the select group would be taking the people's role away. The choir is now well accepted, with its role seen as augmenting the singing of the assembly.

The music sung in this parish is drawn mainly from the hymnal *Gather Comprehensive,* second edition, which contains ritual and service music for Roman Catholic parishes in the United States. It includes contemporary and traditional hymns, folk-style and classical pieces, some of which are piano/guitar-based and others more organ-based. The musician tries to create as much variety as she can within the familiar resources available to the congregation. For example, on Ascension Thursday seasonal texts were sung to the tunes more often associated with "For All the Saints" (SINE NOMINE) and "All Creatures of Our God and King" (LASST UNS ERFREUEN). This worked well, because "they knew the melody, and that was great."

She sometimes likes to go back to choral classics. One Easter the choir sang Randall Thompson's "Alleluia." This year, Mozart's "Ave Verum Corpus" was sung on Holy Thursday, though she says, "We're not a big Latin parish here. The congregation likes to know what they are hearing, and if they are going to pray by listening, they have to know what the words mean." About four times a year, she introduces new music in the hymnal. This exercise evokes a great deal of verbal feedback and dialogue. People from the assembly will say of a musical selection, "That was too hard" or "It's OK."

Contributions of the Congregation

An active liturgy committee meets once a month, and it is here that the formal evaluation of liturgies takes place. In addition to lay parishioners, the committee includes the pastor and the music director. Its purpose is to oversee the worship life of the parish and to do major planning and preparation for the liturgical seasons and other special liturgical celebrations. It also provides ongoing formation for the various liturgical ministers and the parish community at large. The committee does not choose music but evaluates how well the music and liturgy worked together. Their group's work is fairly transparent. Minutes of all the meetings can be accessed on the parish website. The music director admits that she doesn't always agree with some members' liturgical suggestions, but "I'll try anything once and then remember that it didn't work."

The pastor adds:

> Ministry in this parish is very broadly owned by the parish, and the people feel very empowered. There is a dedication to ongoing formation/education among those entrusted with liturgical leadership. There is an open exchange of opinion about matters liturgical, musical, homiletic. There is also a

climate of great hospitality, and a strong tradition of greeting newcomers and visitors. This has the effect of drawing people into the worship that is already in place.

The music director knows that the parishioners appreciate the music—the variety of styles, both traditional and contemporary, and the professional execution of the music. She adds, "People are naturally willing to give money to things that they perceive are valuable and worthwhile."

The parish's main resources are the parishioners and their musicianship, particularly the young people who play instruments. A few parishioners are composers. One man who has a doctorate in composition recently wrote a piece for the eight or nine youth instrumentalists.

Musical Traditions Unique to This Place

The parish has an abundance of traditions. The failure to include certain songs "would cause a rebellion," declares the music director. The assembly knows that some of the musical selections will not change. On Holy Thursday, the congregation always sings "We Come to Your Feast" by Michael Joncas. "All Shall Be Well" by John Foley will "always and forever" be sung as the final hymn on Easter and on Pentecost. During Advent, another John Foley piece, "The Wreath Song," has been sung for years and years at the beginning of mass to accompany the lighting of the Advent candle. During the Easter season, instead of reciting the Creed, the assembly sings "Renewal of Baptismal Promises" by David Haas, with the priest leading the congregational responses, as mentioned previously.

The gathering space is so small that when people walk into the church for the 10:00 a.m. mass, they immediately begin talking to one another. The music director is convinced that if the priest were to get up and say, "During Lent, we're not talking before mass," there would be problems. She sees the gathering hymn as the last part of the gathering rite, which begins naturally as worshipers enter the church.

WHEN THINGS GO WRONG

The musician believes that over time, an assembly comes to trust the leaders to make the right decisions so that the excellence of the worship is maintained. Sometimes adjustments may need to be made quickly during a liturgy. If something goes wrong during a liturgy in this parish, people know that the music director will fix it. The musician explains, "Everybody looks at me. No matter what happens, it's my fault. There is a saying, 'I got *The Look* this mass.' The priest will look over his glasses, which means, 'This isn't working.'" Once, at a wedding, the priest could not be heard because he had forgotten to turn the on-switch for the wireless microphone he was wearing. All eyes were on the music director. She caught the attention of the priest and simply indicated for him to turn it on.

She believes that through music people should be moved to deeper prayer. "If they are distracted, if an organ is blasting or an instrument is too loud and they can't hear each other singing, that is a distraction from prayer. If there is a cantor who is too distracting, I get on it." She gives the example of one cantor who was singing too softly because he wanted to show emotion. However, the assembly couldn't understand all the words—clearly a distraction. So she explained to him that the microphone can do only so much and that he should try to emphasize certain words instead of pulling back.

Sometimes the liturgy committee will suggest something that just doesn't work well in practice. She gave the example of a Palm Sunday procession. For three years in a row, the committee tried having the entire congregation gather in the basement and walk in procession outside, but people were so spread out that it was difficult to keep all the voices together. So at a liturgy committee meeting, she presented a plan to start inside the church. She painted this picture:

> Think of the beautiful scene, with all of the new eco-palms we're using. We will turn around in a sea of new palms, with Father in his bright red vestment up in the loft. We're singing, and Father comes down and processes around the pews. It looks like it did in Jerusalem. The people are standing, watching Jesus; they aren't parading around the city."

People who wanted to join the procession inside the church could do so. The committee approved the idea, and it has worked beautifully ever since.

Can there be too much singing? The music director said that this has happened at two Easter Vigils, when the liturgy was already very long. There was singing during communion and at the post-communion, and then there was a closing hymn. After two or three years, she just didn't schedule so many pieces.

Another suggestion from the liturgy committee that she didn't agree with: that there be only one song for communion. Theoretically, she said, the suggestion might have merit, but once the assembly has sung through the piece twice, and many more are waiting to be served, the introduction of new music gives richness and depth to this important time. She and the committee are still working that one out. The act of communion is special for each person who communes, and the music should reflect the importance of the liturgical moment.

A Parish with a Strong Singing Tradition

The music director says that in this parish, music does not accompany the liturgy but is a vital part of it. New people feel this vitality when they visit the church and are caught up in the active participation of the community. It is evident that she is the driving force behind that active participation. She seems exceptionally attuned to the needs and expectations of both the choir and the assembly, and she is very skilled at leading from the piano.

The pastor, too, recognizes the congregation as a far-above-average singing community. "For them it's an unspoken point of pride. They 'get it' that good worship must involve everybody doing his or her part."

For the approximately thirty years that this parish has been a "parish of choice," it has had pastors who were accomplished singers and musicians. Certain traditions—special songs sung during specific liturgies, some written especially for this parish—are sacrosanct. The priest admits, "This phenomenon was not created by me. The way they do things here is the product of my predecessors. We have a tradition going back decades, and we won't want to lose it." This is a parish that will always sing.

SITTING IN DARKNESS

CHAPTER 4

Quality and Participation Abound, Anglican Style

THIS EPISCOPAL PARISH, FOUNDED IN 1902, IS COMPOSED of 750 families, totaling 2,100 parishioners. The original traditional worship space, built in the early twentieth century, was renovated by adding two wide transepts and moving the altar to the center of the worship space. The result is an open, warm, and inviting atmosphere. The space is beautifully designed and visually uncluttered, with hard surfaces that contribute to vibrant singing. The organ was renovated several years ago, and the pipes were placed so that they speak better into the space. When the organ was shipped to England for renovation, a chamber organ was purchased for use in worship; it remains an important additional instrument for accompanying the liturgy. A seven-foot, six-inch Yamaha grand piano was added to the sanctuary several years ago and is available for performances in the church concert series as well as for worship services. The music program consists of an adult choir, a handbell choir, and a graded children's choir program affiliated with the Royal School of Church Music, a worldwide network of churches, schools, and individuals originating from the Anglican tradition and committed to high-quality music in worship.

The music facilities are upstairs, above the parish hall, and consist of an adult/bell-choir room with risers and tables, director's office and music library, children's choir room, and a classroom that doubles as an area for teaching music skills to the children. An adjacent computer lab provides software programs to teach and reinforce the music curriculum the director has developed for the children's choir program. Parents of the children help with the logistics of this program. For rehearsal, both choir rooms have adequate grand pianos that have recently been refurbished.

The adult choir regularly sings at the 11:00 a.m. service each Sunday, using the Rite I liturgy with traditional plainsong or Anglican chant for psalm settings. The children's choir usually sings at the 9:00 a.m. service using the Rite II liturgy, though these choirs switch roles occasionally. (The traditional Rite I retains older English language from the denomination's 1928 prayer book; Rite II, using updated language, stems from the 1979 revision of the *Book of Common Prayer*.) On feast days, both choirs sing at both services, ably leading the congregation in vibrant singing of psalmody, hymns, and the ritual music. Each year, the adult choir also sings five or six of the monthly services of choral Evensong, and the children's choir sings two or three. A highlight of the music program, in addition to special music on feast days, is the singing of a major Passion at noon on Good Friday, most recently the *St. Matthew Passion* and the *St. John Passion* of J. S. Bach. These Passions require a great deal of preparation and evoke a high degree of anticipation by both congregation and choir. Since 2000, the choir has done three one-week choral residencies in cathedrals in England (Wells, Ely, and Durham), and another is planned.

The Leaders

The current success of the music program flows from the commitment of a former rector who hired the current musician to maintain and further build on an already high-quality music program, the ability of the musician to produce the best of parish music programming, and the continuation of those commitments through subsequent rectors. The musician has been in place through the tenures of three successive rectors; the current rector arrived a few years ago.

Job Descriptions

The priest is the leader of the community and pastor, and is responsible for the financial aspects of the church. Responsibility for the liturgy also resides in his office. He intends his style of ministry to be collegial and collaborative, so that all can bring their best gifts as ministers of the church. He sees himself as a steward of the community, and his goal is to help it grow.

The musician works under the letter of agreement created when he was hired, which asks him to "provide for the musical needs of the parish." That has meant directing three choirs—children's, adult, handbell—and playing two services on Sunday morning and a third once a month and on feast days. He coordinates with the rector in the selection of hymns, consults with the rest of the staff for other musical events, and plays for weddings and funerals.

Musical Formation

The priest has had some musical training via piano lessons and singing in choirs. He grew up in a small Plymouth Brethren church with little formal liturgy but lots of hymn singing. He came to this congregation from a parish in New York City. He appreciates the gifted musician and the program in place for adults and children, acknowledging that this parish appreciates the historical Anglican music tradition. He is interested in church growth and believes it is spurred through the worship service.

The musician grew up in a Methodist church in rural Ohio, where he went to choir practice with his mother. He loved watching the organist. When his parents bought a piano, he began teaching himself to play from some of his mother's piano books. The organist at church asked him to play for her, and when he played a hymn he had learned on his own, she said lessons were in order to develop this natural talent. He started taking piano lessons, then began organ lessons in fifth grade, and played his first church service in sixth grade. By the time he reached high school, the church organist insisted that he study with a better teacher; that, he said, was "one of the most generous things she could have done." By that time, he had a good sense of direction for his undergraduate and master's degrees. He completed his doctorate at a major university in organ and choral conducting, studying under a renowned choral conductor, and was awarded the prestigious Fulbright fellowship to Germany. He formerly worked in a Presbyterian church. He is also the associate conductor of a major symphony chorus. He takes his responsibility to the Anglican musical tradition seriously. He believes that music offered in the worship of God needs to be the very best the church can offer.

Theological Formation and Vocation

The priest describes his Plymouth Brethren background as "low church, free church, no clergy, and with a strong musical tradition." He says church was always important to him, but with a fairly fundamentalist tradition as his background, he was ready for a change by the time he left for college. The Episcopal church on campus at his college was appealing for its architecture, organ, choir, liturgy, and polished language. After college he worked in advertising and commercial art in Manhattan, where he discovered the stunning architecture of an Episcopal church near his workplace. He reflects that several times in his life, "architecture has converted me." He became more involved in the church, explored theological studies, and eventually went to seminary.

The musician came to the church through the music, because the church was the place where he could play the organ and direct choirs, where he found community, and where he could give of his musical gifts. It was later that the mystery and drama of the liturgy gradually led to a "spiritual awakening" that brought theology and music into alignment. It was then that he joined the Episcopal Church.

PLANNING WITH A DIVERSE CONGREGATION IN MIND

Pastor and musician hold planning meetings once a week. The musician plans most of the music, and the discussions are mostly about the choice of hymns. Both priest and musician struggle to serve a congregation that is highly educated but ranges from those who have been Episcopalians since birth to newcomers from evangelical megachurch traditions who know little about Anglican liturgy and music. Priest and musician both acknowledge the importance of engaging all in worship through music, though they approach congregational participation in different ways.

The priest wants to use music already familiar to the people who come to worship:

> I've seen music opening doors for the people's experience of God in worship and also shutting it down. Music can be an obstruction, an impediment to worship. About 40 to 50 percent of our community have not been raised as Episcopalians. So I take it as part of my job not only to include the finest of music in the Anglican tradition, but also to help people from other traditions to "get there," to access it. And that's a big challenge.

The musician sees the Anglican tradition as a rich treasure of liturgy and music and a means for the Episcopal Church—and this particular parish—to make a unique contribution to the faith of those who have chosen to worship in the Anglican tradition. In his view, to diminish the tradition is to create a liturgy with less integrity, to diminish the experience of God that the music of the Anglican tradition can offer to worshipers. So he prefers to help the congregation understand the music, so parishioners can participate fully in its richness. Further, he sees this as his responsibility:

> In the ongoing life of the congregation, the musician can do a lot to help them preserve their own integrity and heritage. The Episcopal Church has a God-given trust of music, a heritage that is so incredible and so rich. My job as an Anglican musician is to help this congregation preserve that. My job as a professional musician and as a musician of the greater church is to honor and continue the development of that tradition.

To achieve this goal, he uses several educational venues:

> We have worship notes in the service leaflet each Sunday. The clergy and I share the writing of the worship notes. Sometimes it's about music, and sometimes the clergy comment on specific liturgies or seasons. One of the things I write about is why we sing what we do. If we're introducing a new hymn, information about the hymn is provided, and perhaps something about the composer, the text, and its origins.

At times a hymn has been taught within the worship service itself, the choir singing through a verse and the congregation singing it back. Sometimes a new hymn is introduced on a given Sunday and then sung on each of the next three or four Sundays.

Sometimes the musician teaches the congregation about the music of worship outside the worship service—for example, during "forum" sessions on Sunday morning or in a Wednesday evening class, especially if there is a special musical event coming such as a Bach Passion. Sunday morning forums have also been used to introduce new settings of service music, educating the congregation on why it is appropriate to enrich each liturgical season with its own music and using the adult choir to help participants learn the next season's music.

Further, the musician takes great care to educate the members of the choirs not only to sing well, but also to understand what they are singing, and he calls for their personal involvement in the music-making:

> We can get the color just right. All of the pitches and rhythms are taken care of, and we can get the intonation to work. At some point, all I have to do is say to them, "I hear this, and it's beautiful, but I don't hear your personal connection to the text." And then they transform it. Then the music just glows and radiates.

VIEWS OF MUSIC IN LITURGY

The priest and musician both see worship as the focal point of the mission of the church and are committed to using the finest of music in the Anglican tradition toward that end. Both regard music as critical to true liturgy and are committed to the ideal of integrating music and liturgy. Their perspectives differ slightly on choice of hymns, with the priest preferring hymns he sees as more accessible to parishioners, and the musician favoring hymns that most closely reflect the lectionary readings. The priest says:

> I'm slightly musically trained—enough to be dangerous, I think. I can read music. I play the piano. I can sight-read and pick things out. I've sung in choirs. But I do take as part of my charge to advocate for people who are not musically inclined, to make sure that their experience of church is not just for the musically literate. So I'm always advocating for singing hymns that are widely known. This is a well-educated crowd. The important thing is that we bring everybody along.

Priest and musician work together until they have achieved something of both of their goals.

The priest sees worship not necessarily as an end in itself but as a means to the growth of the church:

> In the most general sense, I see myself as being a steward of the great gift of this community, and my goal is to help it to grow. I hope it will grow in numbers. I hope it will grow in our ability to give more money away [to charity]. I hope it will grow in the ways that people individually and corporately encounter God—grow in their own understanding of who God is and grow in their own ability to navigate modern life in a faithful way. I think churches are supposed to grow. And when they don't grow, they stagnate. I think a big part of that growth, frankly, comes through the worship experience. I strive to keep that at the center of what we do.

The musician approaches music from a more liturgical, transcendent perspective:

> I think that music has a dominant role in Episcopal liturgy. I believe that the music of worship is meant to give us glimpses of God, a sense that we're part of something that we can't really fathom, to raise us to new levels of understanding, to help us raise our consciousness to God through worship.

He likes the writing of the Lutheran theologian Marva Dawn, who says that the subject and object of worship is God. He worries that we compromise our worship and that it becomes "about us." He believes that God deserves no less than our best: "I often tell the choirs here that if we are going to offer to God in worship, that offering needs to be the best that we can do. It needs to reflect our minds as well as our hearts."

What Makes for a Good Leader?

The priest thinks a good leader is one who has the ability to listen and not get too far out ahead of people, someone who can speak with clarity and who has an idea of where he or she wants to go. He believes that leadership in a church setting is different from the leadership of an ad agency. He quotes a bishop he knows who said, "We want leaders who are happy." He understands that to mean leaders in the church who are centered and at peace with themselves, with personal equilibrium that allows them to be free to lead, and not consumed with their own "drama."

The musician wrestles with the way musicians are educated in relation to what he knows about how church music works. Because he is driven to make the music as meaningful as it can be, he sometimes forgets that he is working with amateur choir singers in a church setting. He tries to take their time seriously:

> I think respect for the time of others is critical. All of my rehearsals begin exactly when I say they'll begin, and they end at the time they're scheduled to end. If I find I really need more rehearsal time, I tell them the week prior that "next week's rehearsal is going to go ten or fifteen minutes longer." That's the only way I'll extend rehearsals. So, "respect for their time" means organization on my part.

He also defines respect as making sure to ask *enough* of singers: "Respect for these people means knowing what they can do and not underestimating them. I think that's very important. They get excited when everything works well. They are profoundly moved by a really beautiful anthem. And they are aware of the effect that can have on those worshiping." Part of the musician's success in leadership is his ability not to diminish the lay musicians or their capabilities by asking too little.

On the Role of the Professional Musician

The priest and musician reflect on what it means to be a professional in a field that is also a religious calling. The priest believes any role in the church is one of servanthood. He has never known any professional musicians in churches who could not have made more money elsewhere, yet they worked for the church because of a calling. He equates musicians serving God through music with clergy who, despite the inherent tensions between being a professional and having a vocation, are helping people encounter God in their own and others' lives.

The musician identifies the core issues of professionalism:

> I think the wise congregation hires what they want for their music program. If they want a better program, then they hire a better musician. If they want a music program that supports and validates worship, then they hire someone who keeps worship as the focus of the music. I think too many congregations just hire somebody to play the keyboard, or somebody who can teach the choir the anthems. But the person they hire does much more than play the keyboard or teach the anthems. The musician helps form who they are as a congregation.

He also thinks it is part of the role of the professional to educate. He cites the choir's experience with Bach's *St. Matthew Passion,* something many in the choir thought they could never master. He said to them, "But you've got me as a director, and I've decided that you can do it." He believes part of the role of the professional to say to the nonprofessionals, "Yes, you can," and to show them how. And when they learned the Bach, it took them to a higher place than they had ever imagined for themselves or for the congregation.

Both priest and musician see music as a powerful tool in the faith development and educational life of the parish. The priest values music for the education of his own children in the faith, as well as for the children in the choir program that the musician directs. He understands that what they are learning is something they will carry with them for life. He also sees the children's choir program as one means of church growth: "Statistics show that children who sing in choirs like this end up finding a home in church. Music is a spiritual device that 'gets into your system.' It becomes part of you and is integrated in a way that just words don't do." He also reflects on the nature of the liturgical year and how it orders life according to the themes of the gospel message. Music helps to tell that story. Living the story over time will be accompanied by spiritual and musical growth. He thinks people come to church for a lot of reasons—and for some, the reason is the call of music.

The musician takes the long view of music's contribution to the life of any congregation: it helps congregants to preserve with integrity some of their lasting traditions. Music accompanies many of the rituals of the church. By preserving the integrity of the music, the church maintains the integrity of the rituals. He acknowledges the difficulty of the task: "It's a rough time, because so much of parish ministry these days seems to be more and more market-driven, and, at some level, the market will sink to its lowest common denominator." This parish is struggling too, though a recent survey of the congregation indicated strong support for music as it is currently being offered: "There is nothing wrong with this. Don't you dare touch it." But people newer to this congregation also said, "We'd like the music to be easier and happier, more 'hip.'" He hopes to help the congregation stay on track.

Full and Active Participation, Anglican Style

The musician applauds the Vatican II goals of full, active, and conscious participation of the laity in worship. He thinks these goals have in many ways been hallmarks of the Episcopal faith for centuries, especially in the parish church (in comparison to the cathedral church where a professional choir offered music on behalf of the congregation). Music has been highly valued in general in the Anglican tradition. It is understood as a vehicle of worship, and the influences of popular styles of music have taken root much more slowly. The service of Evensong in the English cathedrals may be seen as involving the congregation more passively, perhaps, in that the choir is the voice of the congregation and is offering the praise and prayer on behalf of the congregation. "Participation" is defined differently, then, so the congregation should also be actively participating in the worship that is being offered, even if the worshipers are not doing the singing. Whether listening or singing, the participation is to be active.

The musician is committed to congregational hymn-singing and likes to introduce new hymns, especially when they fit the liturgy particularly well. He believes the introduction of new hymns is an occasion when the musician can exercise leadership. The congregation often doesn't want to sing a new hymn that may add enormously to the meaning of the liturgy, and it must be carefully taught so that worshipers can sing it with confidence. He is careful about how frequently he introduces new hymns, making sure that three or four of the five hymns on any Sunday are ones the congregants know well.

The musician keeps an ongoing record of how many times each hymn has been sung in the past few years. He can look at that record and predict which hymns most people are going to be familiar with. But because the congregation is actively seeking new people, a lot of people in this parish may not have a clue about Anglican liturgy. That fact requires more careful choice and presentation of congregational music.

The musician talks about continuing to discern what of the past is worth preserving and how to honor that heritage. Without this discernment, he says, we risk becoming self-absorbed, contemporary people who lose all sense of our past. Part of the richness of the church and its worship is that it goes on and on and on, an idea he finds expressed in the words of one evening hymn:

> We thank thee that thy Church, unsleeping
> While earth rolls onward into light,
> Through all the world her watch is keeping
> And rests not now by day or night.
>
> —JOHN ELLERTON (1826–1893)

The Episcopal tradition includes chants that scholars have traced to the fifth and sixth centuries. Psalm tones are rooted in Hebrew melodies. The musician believes if all that is lost, it is more than the church can afford to leave behind. He laments, "We have to be able to discern what makes sacred music sacred. And that becomes increasingly difficult, because it involves a level of understanding and musical education on the part of the congregation that isn't always there anymore."

The Music Program

The music program is finely honed to serve the liturgical needs of the parish as well as to give young people the musical skills that will create a new generation of musicians to serve the church. The instruments and rehearsal spaces support these goals. Investments have been made in high-quality resources that last. Everything has a purpose; nothing is done frivolously.

Resources

In addition to the beautiful sanctuary, rehearsal rooms, and instruments, a yearly budget of $50,000 supports the music program above the staff salaries. This figure includes $25,000 for four paid singers, and the remainder covers music purchases, instrument maintenance, and extra musicians for special feast days and events. A continuing-education fund for staff members is also provided. When special functions such as the English cathedral trips are planned, support for those expenditures comes from fundraising activities and donations beyond the budget.

Traditions

When the conversation turns to traditions unique to this parish, *quality* as defined by Anglican tradition is a recurring theme. The priest describes a fairly traditional program of Anglican music: "The commitment to the quality is distinctive." The musician observes, "Our parish has long had a reputation for having a good, solid music program, a fairly broad mix of literature within the 'art music' tradition. We do everything from chant to the music of contemporary composers, much of it from the English cathedral tradition." They also use three types of chant—Anglican, simplified Anglican, and plainsong—with all of the choirs, including the children, who can do any of them.

The priest is thinking about new traditions as he begins his tenure in this parish:

> I'm remembering what somebody told me early on, a priest who said that, regarding worship, you should make it your most excellent offering, whatever it is. "Try to be two things: keep it reverent and engaging." There's a lot of engaging worship around that's not really reverent in the sense of being in the presence of God. There's a certain amount of reverence that is not particularly engaging. So those are two poles.

He also talks about "hospitality" for newcomers. How is the music hospitable to people? There are many questions the priest is asking on behalf of this parish, as he considers his agenda a work in progress.

LITURGY AS EDUCATION

The music of the church has much to teach those who sing and experience it. This parish has explored several ways of tapping some of the best of sacred music to teach the faith. From the masterworks of the past to the simplicity of hymns that children can offer, every musical means is used to teach and enrich the spiritual lives of the members.

OFFERING A BACH PASSION

The musician sees his role first as a liturgical minister, providing music for the worship service, and then as an educator of the lay musicians he directs. Singing one of the hallmark Passions of J. S. Bach on Good Friday has served as a musical, spiritual, and liturgical educational experience for the parish. A work originally intended as a liturgical offering by one of the church's great musical theologians, it is now mostly relegated to concert hall performance and is lost for its liturgical value to most worshiping Christian congregations. But not to this one. This congregation and its musicians have found a way to appropriate one of the treasures of the past in a meaningful worship service for Good Friday in a local church. The musician says:

> The *St. Matthew Passion* is a major undertaking for any parish, but especially for a suburban parish with only four paid people in the adult choir. We opted to sing all the biblical portions, plus choruses and chorales, omitting all of the solo arias. The entire work would take three hours, but omitting the solo arias allows it to be offered in less than ninety minutes. We discovered it works surprisingly well this way. Since the solo arias set non-biblical texts, the Passion [biblical] narrative is intensified when it continues uninterrupted, and works beautifully as a Good Friday liturgy.

The choirs have the chance to learn and sing a profound masterwork as a liturgical offering, telling the narrative itself. The children sing the chorales, which Bach intended to be the response of the people to the biblical narrative. Professional guest soloists sing the roles of the Evangelist and Jesus. When these elements are put together, a profoundly moving Good Friday liturgy results. With classes offered to help the congregation and choirs understand the background and meaning of the work, the *St. Matthew Passion* becomes a liturgical ministry for the choirs, and then also for the congregation as the entire church offers it to the greater community.

The musician describes the emotional experience of the day:

> Starting at noon on Good Friday, we begin that three hours "with Jesus." There are people in the choir in tears by the end

of it when they sing the final chorus. The children see how their chorales fit into the story. Peter denies Jesus. The children sing, "Who was it that denied you? I did." Coming out of children's voices, that's pretty powerful, and whether they understand it fully yet or not, they understand this is not just what happened then. This is happening now.

Letters of appreciation arrived from the congregation after the event. One woman said:

> I came because you've done the *St. John Passion* in the past. Afterwards, some people around me left, but many didn't, and I realized I couldn't go. I had to sit in the nave to reflect and meditate. Whatever else I had planned, it just didn't happen, because I needed to be there. It was just so powerful.

It is responses like this that keep the choir repeating a Passion year after year as part of its ministry to the congregation and the larger community.

MINISTERING ABROAD

Many church choirs travel, enjoying a combination of touring and performance. The musician wanted to give such an experience more purpose. When the choir members asked about going to England, the musician said he would like to see them do a residency at a cathedral. The astute choir members understood that meant learning much more literature, doing less sightseeing, and keeping a more focused daily routine. Some choir members had some difficulties with the work schedule on the first residency, but the expectations were clear by the next trip, when they were in residence at Ely. All were aware that they were primarily working, and the choir's commitment paid off. The musician remembers:

> Ely was phenomenal! We sang the bejeebers out of everything. We had people in awe at how powerful the singing was. One of

the canons came up to us and said, "We've had a lot of visiting choirs. You're the top of the lot." Everybody loved being part of it. We had choir members after the final Evensong who just sat in the cathedral for a while, some of them even weeping. It is that sort of transforming experience, which comes from doing the music, holding up the vision for singing great music at a very high standard.

But the residency at Ely wasn't easy for the choir, as the singers had to learn an incredible amount of music. The musician asked them to rise to an ever-higher level of singing, to figure out what the next subtleties of phrasing or color or beauty might be. But when they were done, the smiles were evidence that they were thinking, as the musician said, "We nailed that puppy," and by the end of the week, it was standing room only in the Lady Chapel for the last service.

After the tour was completed, choir members captured some of the Ely experience in a pamphlet, "Ely Remembered." One of the choristers wrote: "In the space of Ely, I breathed in air that had been breathed by countless others over hundreds of years. I breathed in that air, and made sounds and echoes that will reverberate forever, and I left my breath for those that come after me."

The priest on staff who accompanied the group on the trip wrote:

The Spirit prays in us in "sighs too deep for words." This passage from Paul's letter to the Romans expresses the depth and almost heartbreakingly intimate experience of offering prayer in the form of song in this grand stone temple. Just as the Spirit's work is too deep for words, so too is the art, the corporate spiritual practice of music. Like any spiritual discipline, preparation allows the moment of offering to be prayerful. The passerby—cathedral tourist—pressed against the iron gate, yearning for what? God? Held there, glimpsing the Divine, as the Spirit prays in us through song too deep for words.

The musician did not know until later in the week that some had listened intently for quite a while, pressed against the gate, as the choir was rehearsing. "It became an image I treasure," he reminisces, "that our singing of this great music was reaching out and somehow holding even those who didn't come for Evensong. I like to think that they did indeed glimpse the Divine."

AN EDUCATION FOR THE CHILDREN

The children's choir is an after-school, graded program for children in grades three through eight. The weekly, two-hour class includes time to work on building music skills through worksheets and computer games, a snack break, and a seventy-five-minute rehearsal.

The musician remembers an incident from the beginning of his work with the children's choir. He had been hired to restore it to its former quality. The program had become more of a social event than a learning experience. When he became concerned that what he was charged to do was not in keeping with the experience some of the parents seemed to expect for their children, he asked the rector if he had hired the wrong person for the job. The rector validated the musician, who described the conversation like this:

> [He told me,] "You've been hired to raise the level of this music program. You're doing it. Do your job." And he sent me out the door. From then on, it became clear that if something needs to be changed, you have to be careful about how you go about it, but you can't back away from change you understand to be important. And so the children's choir has become something that is very wonderful for many children of this parish.

Several attempts have been made to establish choirs for the high school students, but the conclusion is that children's lives become too complex in high school for them to maintain a commitment to a choir. The congregation has searched for alternatives to involve the students in shorter-term musical commitments. They did form a Compline Choir, inviting anyone who had sung in the children's choir to sing Compline on each of the Sundays of Advent. The group was supplemented with adults, because none of the youth could come for all four Sunday evenings, and a positive intergenerational experience resulted.

The children who graduate from this children's choir often continue singing in school choirs, have lead roles in musicals, and continue to participate in music in college. The local high school choir director can pick them out by their "head voice" sound. When he knows they sang with the program at this church, that they can read well and focus, he takes them into his groups right away.

I encountered a parent who brought her children for a Saturday-morning retreat who offered similar thoughts about the program. She expressed admiration for the gifts of the music director and for the life-shaping experience that her children were having as they learned discipline, developed music skills, and grew in their understanding of the church.

MUSIC AS A FORM OF OUTREACH

The music program's intent to educate and minister extends beyond the local church into the community. Evening prayer is sung once a month and draws singers from outside of the church who participate in the choir. Sometimes professional or good lay musicians will also come to sing special events, such as the *St. Matthew Passion* or a service of lessons and carols, so the music director arranges rehearsals that these musicians can attend.

A concert series of professional music performances in the spring brings in the outside community. The priest sees these concert offerings as part of the growth agenda for the church:

> I do think that this series is distinctive. It's a good model of how to provide excellent music in a context that is specifically non-worship. The value of it is that it draws people into our

community that would not probably otherwise come, and
says, "This is a place where you are welcome."

The musician believes the singers are proud of the quality of
the music at the church, but the reputation they have among
outside professionals is not the primary factor in their participation. Members of the church see their service as musicians
as a part of their belonging to the community of faith. One of
the choir members expresses why it is important for her to be
in a choir:

> Since earliest memory I've delighted in music. Musical ability
> and enjoyment are God-given gifts, I believe—and as such are
> intended to be shared. I share the gift by joining with others
> in the church choir. Well-presented, music—like dreams—
> reaches into our core, our soul. It's like St. Paul's depiction of
> the Holy Spirit translating our sighs and groans into prayers.
> But sounding better.

These choir members give enormous amounts of their time to
serve as leaders in worship, working toward high performance
standards, all the while seeing what they are doing as part of
their responsibility and as an offering of their gifts to the church
and to God.

WHAT CAN HAMPER EFFECTIVE MUSIC LEADERSHIP?

For the priest, music choices are a matter of practicality, "what
works." He believes there is an inherent tension between clergy
and musicians about style and quality of music because of music's subjective nature. He elaborates:

> You're dealing in aesthetics. Sometimes what matters deeply
> to some doesn't matter to others. You navigate that by stay-
> ing in touch, staying in conversation, trying to keep your eye

on the prize of what this is all about—worship. I studied fine art for a while. There are times when I have seen things in a church that are visually "assaulting." I can translate that to how a musician, who is much more deeply trained than I am, might feel that same kind of assault and who might say, "I can't deal with that music."

The musician talks about accepting limitations in working with volunteer musicians. He says:

Part of leadership is accepting that there are going to be limits. There are times when I feel that I've been compromised, or the choir has, or an anthem has been compromised because of something that has happened. That is the nature of church music. So you back up, regroup, and try to make it clearer next time. Oftentimes it's a lack of understanding.

Then the musician speaks about a particular instance when he realized that the music had changed from an offering to a performance, perhaps even to entertainment, which troubled him more than a little. In June the liturgy sometimes has included more informal music. One year music from the gospel tradition was used. The congregation applauded—in this parish, an unusual response. The reaction brought troubling questions for the musician: "Was it received as entertainment? Is the applause why we sing? Are we going to replace more substantive music with music that receives applause?" He is still seeking answers to these questions.

About the Congregation

Because there is no formal liturgy or music committee, it may be difficult to pinpoint ways the congregation gives input to the music program. But on closer examination, one sees that the influence of the congregation is profound. Congregational singing is robust in all quarters of the sanctuary at both services. In the 11:00 a.m. service where Rite I is used, many in the congregation sang the Psalm using traditional Anglican chant printed in the bulletin, a daunting challenge for any congregation. The number attending the Good Friday Passion is significant, and their reverence indicates that this is a meaningful experience, many coming early and staying long after the service ends. The choir's mission to provide music for the liturgy of the hours in cathedrals of England is partially supported by a fundraising "hymnathon," for which parishioners pledge to pay a certain amount per hymn as the choir sings through the entire hymnal. A lay committee was formed to organize and present the afternoon concert series, an outreach to the community. The development and maintenance of the music facilities, instruments, and libraries are clearly the result of resources the congregation makes available for the best of their kind. Congregational feedback to the staff, musicians, and clergy makes evident members' pride in, and support of, their music program.

Parish publications say, "Worship is at the center of all we do here." The beautiful space, the fine pipe organ, the resources to maintain the music-making enterprise all point to congregational support of a liturgical worship style that is faithful to the Anglican heritage. The worship is dignified and lectionary-based, and all of the music is carefully selected to relate to the lessons of the day. For those who sing or play in the service, their musical offerings are part of their worship. Likewise, the congregation understands its role in supporting the music leaders but also in participating fully in the sung congregational portions of the service.

Shortly after the new rector arrived a few years ago, a congregational survey was taken to acquaint the rector with congregational views on a number of matters. A few of the questions were about worship. Responses indicated a high degree of satisfaction with worship. Those new to the church who come from non-Episcopal backgrounds often have chosen this church because of the mystery and dignity of the worship, yet they don't always understand what it is that makes Anglican worship what it is. The question is how to bring together a congregation of lifelong Anglicans with those new to Anglicanism.

Reaching Back and Moving Forward

This church maintains an awareness of its history, treasures its solid foundations, and moves forward with wisdom and thoughtful, generous openness to share its riches with all who have interest. Grounded in the finest of Anglican traditions, the parish holds firmly to its roots while asking how to respond to seekers who are attracted to the mystery of these traditions and yet sometimes confused by them. The musician, who has been in place during the ministries of three rectors, has built a program of quality of which the congregation is justifiably proud. A children's program serves the church well. A volunteer adult choir gives many hours in ministry. Congregational participation in services is vital. A relatively new rector is committed to growth. The musician holds the richness of the Anglican musical and liturgical tradition as a treasure and offers education to congregants to help them gain access to these spiritual resources. The rector appreciates the fine liturgical and aesthetic resources of Anglicanism and sees them serving worship, the centerpiece of the church's mission. He and the musician work together to find ways to use the riches of the tradition and to make them available to all the congregation, whether cradle Episcopalians or seekers.

The Saviour

CHAPTER 5

Mission and Music
Intertwine in Diversity

By Linda J. Clark

HERE WE VISIT AN EPISCOPAL CHURCH LOCATED IN A CON-
glomeration of cities, suburbs, and towns spreading west from
a major East Coast city. The congregation was founded as a
mission station of a nearby congregation in the mid-nineteenth
century. The present building, completed at the turn of the last
century, matches in style other large churches in the area. The
building itself is beautiful. The sanctuary is large, but warm and
inviting. It has a wooden ceiling with beams and arches. A small
clerestory in the middle allows natural light to fall on the pews.
There is a center aisle, as well as two side aisles.

The congregation is ethnically and socioeconomically
diverse, with a significant segment from the islands of the Caribbean. Its mission history is at the center of its present identity:
it supports a soup kitchen, a kids' co-op, and other outreach
programs for people of the area. The congregation numbers 350
or more, and attendance on Sundays ranges from 150 to 200,
from the very young to the very old. I visited on Confirmation
Sunday, and the bishop was expected. As the time for worship
neared, the sanctuary was filled with "tweens," teens, and many
family members.

I had found a parking space about a quarter-mile away.
Walking from there to the church through an ethnically diverse

urban area, I passed Thai, Japanese, and Indian restaurants; pizza parlors; an Indian clothes shop; pubs; a psychic advertising tarot-card readings; and other businesses. At a little square, a police officer was waking homeless people, and a priest and others were serving coffee and doughnuts to the gathered population. The neighborhood is a good example of the emerging "minority-majority" demographic of American society.

Walking into the church for the first time, I felt that I had entered a different world. I went from a busy commercial street into a beautiful ecclesiastical space. As I learned more about the congregation, I recognized that it was a space where the homeless people down the street would be welcomed both at Sunday services and during the week at the various meals served and the food pantry.

Both the history and location of this church are essential in understanding the kind of music ministry found there and the rationales that both priest and musician provide for their work. As the rector commented in an interview:

> The musical leadership of the congregation is going to depend upon the environment of the congregation, and by that I mean the sociological and geographical environment. What can be perfectly appropriate and wonderful for [us] might not be appropriate and wonderful for another church. So if we're not aware of our environment, in terms of the people who live in our neighborhood, the people who worship with us, then we're not going to accomplish a great deal. I have a friend who says, "If your congregation doesn't look like your neighborhood, there's a problem with the congregation."

The congregation would agree with the rector's expressed sentiments, and its mission endeavors in the area are consistent with these principles and those of the church's history going back to the English Tractarian movement of the nineteenth century.

The Leaders

The priest is the rector of the parish and is responsible for the spiritual life of the congregation. Along with the vestry—the lay governing body—he administers and oversees the parish's various programs. The musician, a half-time employee, is responsible for providing music at the various parish activities. His main responsibility is worship on Sunday. There is also a part-time religious educator on the staff. The success of the leadership of priest and musician flows, among other things, from their musical and pastoral formation and their common understanding of their work. The priest has a strong musical background and sings well. The musician brings a pastoral lens to what he is doing. Each functions within his own sphere of training but can understand and appreciate what the other is doing. Their work together has not been conflict-free, but they have come to a working consensus on most aspects of their common tasks.

THEIR FORMATION

The priest grew up in England. Throughout his childhood he was involved in choral singing and music-making. He listened to and sang with hymn-singing programs broadcast on the radio every Sunday night. As a youth, he took part in nationwide choral programs. Raised in a Methodist/Plymouth Brethren milieu, he was initially attracted to evangelical forms of worship but then settled into the Anglican Church. However, as he was quick to point out to me, he has never lost his fondness for more evangelical forms of music-making, particularly strong congregational singing.

The musician was raised Catholic and trained in piano performance at a state university in the Midwest. He did a lot of choral singing in university and took jobs in local churches to work his way through school. To do these jobs, he learned skills for being a church musician: conducting, hymn writing, organ playing.

The musician has been at the church for more than twenty-five years, having arrived in 1983. He has a reputation in the area for developing the music program in this church. He is also an excellent hymn writer. The quality of music in this congregation's worship derives in part from the creation of several resources and practices that give voice to the people. During his long tenure at the church, he has helped compile a hymnal supplement; he has also fostered the writing and use of a group of psalm settings and refrains composed by congregants and members of the choir.

THEIR WORK TOGETHER

In the role of music in the liturgy, one can see the way these two men complement each other. The priest remarked, "[Music's] the way in which congregations can be united, stretched, taught, and joyful." He values the way music can deepen faith:

> Thanks to [the musician,] we're ready to learn new things here, and we're ready to go back to some very old things. Last Sunday they sang a seventeenth-century Anglican anthem—classical Anglican—as an offertory. To see and to hear the choir sing something from the classical tradition, and then a little later singing music from Zambia—it's one of the wonderful gifts we have here. We haven't forgotten the heritage, but we've broadened and extended it, so that we're not stuck in a cultural warp, and that would be my strongest criticism of some Anglican music.

The priest's focus is on the congregation. For example, he understands how difficult it can be to make a transition between the chaos of getting to church and becoming engaged in worship. The pivotal point is the opening hymn, which should be a familiar one:

The people come in hustling and bustling, hurried and late, with all kinds of worries and joys. The transition from the street and the home to assembly of worship is a difficult one, and at that point, I want them to have something that enables people to say, "It's all right. It's OK. I'm here; I remember now. I was here last Sunday, and I'm back again."

The musician has a similar focus on the congregation:

If there weren't music, I couldn't go to church. It's a special part of being together. I'm constantly paying attention to whether a song went well—whether people sang it. And that's as important an indicator of what's going on as anything else. People who have never sung in a group before can come to church and do that.

He is also keenly aware of the need for music to address concretely the lives of the people in the congregation:

[I work to provide] an opportunity for people to come together on a weekly basis and share such an intimate thing as singing together. Sometimes it's enough to keep people going. They remember what they sang, and it comes back to them during the week.

The lay leader I interviewed had a similar view of the role of music in worship. She commented that music unites and binds in both formal and informal ways. It has so many facets—praise, lament, awakening—that "everyone can find the spark within." The musician has a unique way of drawing people into music. "He gives voice to those who have no voice or who are hurting or are timid."

The priest echoed this emphasis on the connection between worship and ordinary life:

There is a liturgical piety that says, "We expect something to happen here today that will speak to our lives—the world we live in, to make the connection between what we're doing as a people of God here on Sundays and what we're doing as a people of God Monday through Saturday." Church for most of the congregation is not an excursion out of the busy world. It's a place where people begin to make sense of their busy lives and worlds. Too many hymns talk about how awful we are, how wonderful God is, and how great it will be when we'll all be in heaven. We don't like hymns that always end in heaven. This congregation was born in a mission, and lives by a mission, and exists for a mission, and that is a tradition that we have continued.

This is a congregation whose worship is linked to members' daily lives. Their worship is a means of completing who they are and offers a way to make sense of the complex world they live in. Worship focuses them, nourishes them, and provides an opportunity for them to serve one another and the world beyond their own congregation.

Concept of Good Leadership

Priest and musician are colleagues; both expressed trust in the other's work. "We read each other well," the priest remarked. Although the polity of the Episcopal Church specifies that the rector is responsible for worship, that hierarchical structure does not impede their work together. They have similar goals for the music in the liturgy. There have been times when they disagreed but conscientiously met to work things out, learning from each other. Both explicitly spoke of the necessity for the "back-and-forth" work they do together.

The priest has a good understanding of how to work with others, gleaned from experience. He recalls:

I was in a congregation where a musician refused to play certain music, and I thought that was unacceptable. And her inability to negotiate around that made it very difficult for me. I've also been "the bad rector" who has ridden hard on the musicians and said, "We'll do *this*."

He believes that in the best of circumstances the musician and the rector see some kind of common service. He has learned that both leaders can enhance and support each other, or they can destroy each other.

The musician brings a pastoral understanding to his work with the congregation and the various musical organizations in the church. To him, leadership is measured by the degree to which people assume responsibility for their own faith journeys: "I read something that said that people's response to good leadership is, 'Well, we just did it ourselves.' So it means empowering people to own what they need to, and to move in the direction that they need to."

The musician understands his vocation as promoting the singing of the congregation. He points to the work of one of his mentors, John Bell, a minister of the Church of Scotland known internationally for his skill as a song leader: "That's what I want to do. That's what the church needs—someone to stand up before people and unabashedly get them to sing, and form their own theology and enjoy it."

Planning

The priest and musician hold planning meetings approximately once a month, more frequently when necessary. These meetings may also include the Christian education staff member. Informal evaluation goes on continually. The evaluative phrases that each of them frequently used were "This worked" and "Why didn't this work?"

On occasion a formal worship-and-music committee is organized. There is also a worship group in the vestry (parish governing board), which focuses promarily on ushering and the mechanics of worship. The vestry might discuss how to enrich worship, or the priest might give vestry members a "heads-up" about aspects of worship coming up.

When the collaborative model of leadership so ably demonstrated in this church is ignored, as it was in an experiment called "Whole Community Sunday," things go awry. Noting that in all of it, the staff never consulted the teachers or the congregation, the priest remarked:

> For three years, we experimented with "Whole Community Sunday." We decided that after the processional hymn there would be a discrete experience for children, which usually involved their coming up and sitting up front on a rug that we had for that purpose. In retrospect, it was a terrible decision. It became "check-out time" for parents. The church-school people were mad because they didn't have enough teaching time. They ended up with children who were unhappy, parents who were unhappy, and a congregation that was unhappy.

This example stands in stark contrast to the collaborative work the musician has done with members of the congregation and choir to compose music for singing psalms. Active involvement in leadership is part of the ethos of this congregation.

The Congregation's Involvement in Musical Leadership

In any church, the priest and musician do not operate in a vacuum. As was pointed out in the introduction, liturgy is "the work of the people." Thus, communication between staff and congregation is a key to success. We asked the priest and musician a series of questions about the congregational milieu in which they work and how it affected their endeavors. The musician reported that, early in his ministry, the choir expressed a desire to "build things up." As a church, the singers wanted to grow; they were open to doing new things to accomplish that aim. This attitude spilled over into the entire congregation, which increasingly supported the work of the musicians by joining with them.

The eclectic musical repertoire developed by the choir and other musicians promoted the growth of the congregation within its increasingly multicultural environment. A diverse group of people found an "aural home" there and an invitation by staff, choir, and congregation to join in the fun. The musician contrasted two approaches to the music of the church:

1. Do lots of different things by many people. Reach out and let people try things. It's all right not to wait for the perfect rendition to act.
2. Do fewer things with well-trained people, but do them well. Wait until you can really do something well.

He tends toward the first option—to involve all kinds of people in the music program. He believes that singing is the most meaningful thing that people do in worship and that he can make "musicians" out of everyone who enters his sphere. "If you have something to offer, you can offer it," he remarked. He approaches new people in the congregation and asks them to do things. He listens to people when they make suggestions and provides opportunities for them to realize their ideas. The priest remarked, "He has the imagination and gift to instill confidence in people. 'You can do it!'"

The constituency of the congregation supports the kind of work the musician wants to do. A diverse and musically talented group of people is attracted to this church. Congregants have to pass by many other churches to get to this one. They have a strong sense of who they are and like the diversity of styles of music. A woman I greeted during the Peace at the church told me that she was a congregant because of the musician.

The Music Program

The church has an adult choir, two choirs for children and youth, a men's chorus that is self-governed and self-directed, and a large group of instrumentalists who play preludes and postludes and accompany congregational singing. As a rule, the choir sits among the congregation until the Passing of the Peace, at which point the singers gather in the front. On the Sunday I attended, music from the Vivaldi *Gloria* and a Buxtehude organ prelude mingled with hymns and chants. Several texts from John Bell were used, set to music familiar to the congregation. The instruments used were also diverse: organ, piano, and percussion instruments accompanied anthems and congregational singing. A Zambian setting of the Lord's Prayer, beloved by the congregation, was accompanied by drums. The last hymn, Sidney Carter's text "One More Step," set to music by the American composer and organist Philip Dietterich, is found in the parish's hymnal supplement.

Lots of people joined enthusiastically in the singing. A newer resource from the national church publishing house—*Lift Every Voice and Sing II,* an African-American collection including hymns and service music—resides in the pews alongside the hymnal supplement and *The Hymnal 1982,* official hymnal of the Episcopal Church. These resources are used throughout the Service of the Word and the Eucharist prescribed in the *Book of Common Prayer.* African music is popular, as is the hymnody of many members' Caribbean heritage. When a congregant made a trip back to the Islands, the musician asked him to bring back a representative collection of hymns to add to the repertoire of the congregation.

In his work with the choir, he advocates training the singers so that their skill level improves. He teaches sight-singing and ear-training in rehearsals. He also offers an occasional voice lesson. "I consider the choir to be the 'yeast' of the congregation."

His musical resources in the congregation include professional instrumentalists. He remarked, "I don't really go out looking to bring in other trained musicians, because we have people here who can do things." An example was a production of *Amahl and the Night Visitors*, by Gian Carlo Menotti. They did not hire musicians, but gathered the ones in the congregation and talented local friends.

The congregation's hymnal supplement has gone through several editions. The first was collected and put in the pews in 1984. The second and third editions followed in 1992 and 2000. The rector, members of the vestry, the choir, and a committee representative of the congregation helped gather the music. There are now seventy selections in it—chants, older favorite hymns not included in the 1982 hymnal, newer hymns that have come on the scene since publication of the 1982 hymnal, service music, and a variety of "world music" songs to reflect the ethnic mixture of the congregation and neighborhood. The arrangements feature organ and piano as well as other diverse instrumentation. In the collecting of this resource, the musician received permission to publish the music. The church subscribes to CCLI and OneLicense.net, licensing agencies that charge an annual fee to grant congregations permission to reprint hymns still under copyright.

When I asked the musician if holding together so many styles of congregational music is difficult, he explained that what causes things to fall apart is using too much *new* music. If the worshipers know the music, the liturgy moves well through the shifts. No one seems to notice them. He teaches the new music through short congregational rehearsals just before worship and the effective placement of the various choirs in the congregation. At the beginning of his tenure, he scheduled potluck suppers and hymn sings to introduce the hymnal supplement, a process he also used to acquaint the congregation with *The Hymnal 1982* when it appeared. In the confirmation service I attended, the congregation was familiar with most of the music and joined in enthusiastically.

At the time of the site study, the musician's compensation as a part-time employee was $30,254. It included salary and a stipend in lieu of benefits such as health insurance and retirement pension, He is also on the staff of a nearby seminary. The church budget for music and liturgy was $3,600.

THE CONGREGATION'S PSALMS

The hymnal supplement, the choirs, and the instrumental ensembles all provide avenues for the congregants to add their voices to those of the leadership on Sunday morning. One of the most successful avenues is the congregational psalm responses. Before the updating of both the prayer book and the hymnal, the psalms were spoken in most Episcopal churches. In the spirit of renewal, the musician decided to try singing the psalms. The choir attempted several forms, and choir members ended up composing their own settings! The musician explained:

> In choir rehearsal, I'd say, "Here's our list of psalms for the next two or three months. Sign up for one and write a refrain. Pick a part of the psalm that you think would work as a good refrain. Write something for it, or sing it, and I'll write it down for you." It was so moving to sing a psalm when it was "hot off the press."

The musician noted that this practice had come up in a time when the idea of composing music was common among the choir members. Although that practice has lessened, the congregational practice of singing these settings has persisted.

About Vatican II

This research project is based on goals set forth by Vatican II for music and liturgy: to promote the "full, conscious, and active participation" of the people and for music to form "a necessary and integral part of the solemn liturgy." We chose this congregation as a model of leadership because of the musician's reputation of engaging the congregation musically in the liturgy. The relationships he developed with priest, choirs, and congregation and the resources he created specifically for this congregation encourage full participation in worship and the integration of music and liturgy. Choir rehearsals often contain group evaluation: "How are we doing?" As a result of his creating an avenue for response, everyone has the potential to be a teacher as well as a learner. An example is his method of dealing with new hymnody, which expands the congregation's vocabulary about God. He gives everyone a chance to voice enthusiasm, reservations, and opposition. This two-way street gives people a forum to speak about their faith, commitments, doubts, and disagreements. By speaking out, they take responsibility for their beliefs. In these exchanges, the musician becomes a spiritual leader in a collaborative venture.

In answer to a question about the values espoused in the various Vatican II documents, the priest related them to the relationship between pastor and musician. "The goal that music forms a necessary or integral part of the solemn liturgy can only be achieved if the pastor and the musician view themselves as partners and not as rivals." He then spoke of the necessity to view their work within the context of the congregation's activity as musicians. "It can only happen if the principal musician sees the other musicians as partners in his [or her] ministry." He occasionally attends the Sunday rehearsal just before church begins:

> There is never the sense that "This is something you are doing for me." There is always the sense that this is something we are doing together and with the congregation. That creates a sense of partnership—between the rector and the musician, between the principal musician and the other musicians, and between the principal musician and the congregation. Partnership, partnership, partnership.

And God Is in the Midst of Them

This model of church music leadership is based on three goals inherent in this church's ministry. The first is the leaders' recognition that what goes on in church has to be explicitly connected to the complex world in which the congregation lives. The second gets back to the values of Vatican II. The participation of the faithful in worship is essential to the connection between worship and world. The third is the understanding that music opens wide the gate to that full and active participation. Few would argue with those aims, and most churches strive for them. How they are carried out in this church with its diverse congregation and its strong focus on mission differs from how that happens in many other places.

The musician talks about the aims of worship planning as focused on the people who are there: "Their hope or expectation of having an encounter with the Divine in a way that is very down to earth. What we're trying to do is nourish each other in honest ways, where we can talk about who we really are."

The priest reiterated these aims but emphasized the mission history of the parish: "Both of us think of the possibility of [inward] spiritual growth for the individual, but never allow that at the expense of the call to be the salt and the light in a world that needs both salt and light."

Standing in the midst of a diverse, commercial neighborhood with its doors wide open, this church, its staff, and the congregation live out their mission origins in very modern guise. What sounds forth from it are the voices and instruments of its gathered flock—all of them! Following the English Reformation's call to provide resources of the living faith in the vernacular and the biblical injunction to serve the poor, the church's musicians have built a musical vocabulary for worship that beckons all to come join them: "You are welcome here!"

This congregation is living out its mission history in the present, bringing the complexities of daily life into worship, its members singing their way into encounter with God and one another, and emerging as whole people. Their offerings are as diverse as the people themselves, given as they are but with hopes for who they want to be. Song unites all who come, and God is found in the midst of them.

Sing

CHAPTER 6

A Choir School
Redefines a Congregation

THIS EPISCOPAL CATHEDRAL IS LOCATED IN AN OLD CITY center where a declining congregation is concerned with the typical stereotypes of an inner-city church: the church was formerly a vital religious and community center with an active boys' choir school and a busy liturgy schedule. More recently, the building and neighborhood had fallen into disrepair as economic hard times befell that area of the city. A decade before this study, a new dean, the priest in charge of the cathedral and its environs, came to the cathedral with a vision to renew the church and its mission by resurrecting the choir school. She hired a musician with a doctorate in music who shared her vision, and the work began. An after-school program now draws children from families of all socioeconomic and racial backgrounds, both from miles away and within walking distance of the cathedral. Vandalism is no longer a problem—the neighborhood feels ownership for the property and helps to care for it.

The structure has always been in some ways unremarkable, with the inherent drawbacks of a stone building built in the mid-nineteenth century and enlarged to respond to immediate needs rather than with a coherent architectural plan in mind. The sanctuary is awkward, with organs in front and rear, neither of which is placed or designed well to support singing. The chancel area absorbs sound, so choirs cannot be heard fully when situated there. Yet these difficulties seem unimportant in light of the high energy and superb quality of the music made in these spaces. The place is less important than what happens in it, and the reverberant acoustics in the nave are used to full effect when the congregation sings.

The dean who envisioned revitalization of the choir school is no longer at the cathedral. A long-term interim dean has been named who has deep roots in the diocese, supports the vision for the cathedral, and is well prepared to lead it into the next stage of its life. Meanwhile, the choir school continues to thrive. The after-school program provides private music lessons and academic tutoring for the children enrolled in the school, as well as a structured mentoring program for life skills. The choir school has enlivened the congregation, with families of children in the school now attending worship and participating in other cathedral activities.

The Leaders

This is an exciting time for the cathedral church. A decline has been reversed, and new energy is evident in the church's daily activities. It is too soon for new ideas to have settled into a comfortable pattern, however, so the leadership is crucial to provide a continuity of vision for this period of growth.

CURRENT JOB DESCRIPTIONS

Having previously served this diocese, the priest has returned from the deanship of another cathedral. As interim dean, he will be here for two to four years as chief pastor, worship leader, and administrator—all the things a rector does while in charge of an Episcopal parish. He will also help the cathedral congregation envision its future and determine what kinds of resources—financial, people, priestly—it will need to make that vision a reality. The music program falls under the jurisdiction of the rector or dean of any Episcopal cathedral or parish, but the canons of the church also instruct the priest to work in collaboration with the musician. The dean explains that he recognizes and honors the musician's gifts and talents, giving him a major leadership role for music. The two of them have an understanding that on some occasions the dean may want to give input or direction, and that is to be honored and respected as well.

The musician has two roles, as canon precentor (the primary cantor/music leader of the cathedral) and as artistic director of the choir school. He has oversight of all the music but acknowledges the authority of the dean and says they work collaboratively in planning liturgy. He also directs choirs—men and women, trebles (children), and teen boys—as separate groups, and together as the Cathedral Choir. He says his work with the congregation and the adults in the choir is the same as it might be in any organist/choir director position, but as director of the school, he spends a significant amount of time training young people.

Early Musical Formation

The dean has been part of a worshiping community since age five. His experience makes it difficult for him to view liturgy without music. "I recognize that while liturgy may be *valid* without music, it is *lacking* without music. Music brings a whole new dimension into the liturgical experience of the congregation that informs, inspires, lifts up, and empowers it."

He is honest about his own musical skills, acknowledging that he is not a great musician. He recalls taking trumpet lessons in fifth grade for five months—until baseball season started, putting an end to the trumpet lessons. But he has always enjoyed music and listens to it a lot. "I find that, depending on my mood, it can be stimulating, calming, uplifting, thought-provoking." So while he has very little formal training, he has a deep appreciation of music. After forty-three years in the ministry, he is well acquainted with hymnody and liturgical music.

Neither of the musician's parents were musicians, but his aunt was a church organist. The musician was raised in the Methodist Church. In elementary school he took acoustic guitar lessons for three years but was drawn to the keyboard. After taking organ lessons with a local teacher, he was sent by the teacher to a nearby college, where the professor said he needed to study piano. Though an organ major in college, he continued piano study through his undergraduate years, which he does not regret. He holds master's and doctoral degrees in organ performance.

AN EARLY SENSE OF VOCATION

The dean was baptized in an Episcopal parish church. His mother and her family were all Episcopalians but were not very active. He tells of a time when he was five years old and an aunt, who was also his godmother, decided that something ought to be done about his religious training. The nearest place was a Methodist church, which he attended for several years. One day on the playground in elementary school, a class friend asked if he went to Sunday school. He told her a fib and said he didn't. This incident turned out to be "life-changing" in many ways because she went back to the little parish his mother had begun to attend and told the young vicar that she knew a little boy who wasn't going to Sunday school. One Saturday morning, there was a rap on the door, and there stood the vicar. He had come to find out about this little boy who didn't go to Sunday school. So the boy found his way back to the Episcopal Church and soon was an acolyte and later a lay leader. In his junior year of college, he considered several options, including the priesthood, but also journalism, law, and politics. He was keenly interested in politics and still is. But in the process of discernment, the priesthood kept rising to the top. So he talked to his parish priest and then to the bishop of the diocese, and after college graduation he went to seminary.

The dean believes informal education through summer jobs during his college years prepared him in special ways for ministry:

> I worked as an electrician's helper and in factories that made milk cartons and aluminum cans. Since I went right from college to seminary, these were the closest I had to "real world experiences." I lived and worked with people of all backgrounds, races, educational backgrounds, and social outlooks. It gave me an understanding of what it is like to live from paycheck to paycheck, to be willing to work sixteen-hour days when the opportunity came along because there may be a day when you might not work at all. People would talk about their family problems in the lunchroom. For me, it was an education.

The musician began playing for church regularly at age thirteen. During college he played for a Presbyterian church, during master's degree work he played at a Unitarian church, and during doctoral work he played at a Lutheran church. Then he took a full-time job in a Presbyterian church that established an after-school choir school program that still exists. It was an exciting time and helped him know that he wanted to train children. But he also sensed that he wanted to do that training in an Episcopal tradition because the choir-school heritage was "tailor-made" for such training. When the cathedral job became available, he applied; he feels blessed to have it. Here he can realize his passion to train young people in the Episcopal tradition, which he considers "such a rich, artistic venue."

Their Understanding of Their Work

The experienced dean, who is new to the cathedral, and the younger musician, who has been in this place for several years, are discovering ways of working together in leading the cathedral's worship. Their mutual respect and collegiality are important at this stage of the cathedral's life, given its new directions and opportunities in motion that are not yet solidified.

PLANNING

Planning for worship is done by the dean and the music director in weekly sessions where they review last Sunday's liturgy and talk about upcoming liturgies. The musician generates the hymn list and gives it to the dean, who reviews it and makes any changes. The dean says, "And if there is some question about it, we'll talk about it. I'll say, 'Here is the reason why I'd like to have this hymn.' It's not just a whim." With an additional half-time priest who occasionally presides, the dean takes the responsibility for scheduling the preaching and celebration of the Eucharist.

The musician praises the rich assets the Episcopal tradition offers for planning a service, with the lections, prayer book, hymnal, and many other Episcopal musical resources that support the liturgical calendar. He appreciates this structure, which makes the job easier, and he enjoys creating a beautiful service. "You want people to be unaware of the pieces, for it to be seamless. To be a part of liturgical planning, where you can create something that really holds together, is a joy."

VIEWS OF MUSIC IN THE LITURGY

The dean finds several purposes for music in Anglican liturgy—namely, to lift the spirit of the worshiping congregation, to offer prayer through song, to enrich the liturgy itself, and to serve as a vehicle for the words of the hymns and the anthems. He considers the anthem to be a second sermon. While he believes music in liturgy should be a gift to both God and the people, he thinks it also should offer an opportunity for the people to express themselves: "That's why I think hymns are so vitally important. They are not 'fill-ins,' but rather an opportunity for the people to express their faith, hopes, and aspirations, to give glory to God, and to petition God."

He also reflects on the additional gift of music that the choir school brings to the congregation. He sees the school as providing a way for the children and young people to enter into the liturgy, not just as participants but as leaders. They are critical to the entire liturgical event. "It's not as if the children come in once a week and practice and every fourth Sunday they sing a little anthem on the chancel steps. Here, it's Sunday after Sunday after Sunday. They are integrally involved in the worshiping life of this congregation." He sees them as ministers among and to the congregation.

The musician points to the formative function of participating in the music of liturgy, particularly for the children in the choir school. He cites the spiritual formation that takes place through the singing of psalms every Sunday or hearing the stories and music of the Easter Vigil, for example. And the children stay involved even after they graduate. Some come to worship in the summer when their parents don't come. Week after week they experience the liturgy and the sermon and sense they have become a part of the church community.

A Good Leader Is . . .

The dean speaks about leadership from his extensive life experience, and sees leadership for music ministry much the same as for pastoral ministry:

> A good leader is one who energizes those he or she is attempting to lead, who leads by direction and by example, who is open to critique and respectful of the opinions of others. A good leader can recognize and follow the leadership of others. A good leader is one who is willing to take the responsibility that goes with leadership, is willing to stretch herself or himself in that role, and is willing to risk calling others to stretch themselves.

He acknowledges that musical expertise is a "given" for music leaders and that leadership of children requires a "special little niche in dealing with young people—a sense of appreciation for their work, and a sense of joy that comes with seeing them blossom and grow, so that your face lights up when their faces are lit up."

In working with adults, the dean believes self-confidence is needed to say, "I am the leader, and I'm called to bring these pieces together." He likens a leader of adults to the conductor of a symphony whose individual players and instruments must be brought together into a single piece of music played in accord. He sees the church choir director similarly, as one who brings individual voices together in a whole, so that the choir can provide leadership and inspiration for the worshiping congregation.

The musician first talks about the leadership training under development for the children in the choir school in partnership with the YMCA. Besides learning how to lead others, the children will be trained in personal leadership and the idea that "if you're tired, you're still going to give your professional best."

The musician sees several forms of musical leadership at work in the cathedral's music program. First, the choir provides leadership for the congregational singing. Second, four section leaders in the choir serve as mentors for the soprano, alto, tenor, and bass sections. Third, adult choir members volunteer as leaders for the choir-school children's activities. Finally, the dean's leadership is critical in providing an overall vision and support for the music program. Further, the ability of the dean and the musician to work together is important for the music program to function as part of the cathedral's mission and to support worship. The musician believes he and the dean share a vision, and he feels blessed to have worked with supportive clergy in his professional roles at the cathedral.

ON THE ROLE OF THE PROFESSIONAL MUSICIAN

The dean believes whether the musician is a volunteer amateur or a paid professional, he or she is owed respect. The volunteer musician's skills most likely will not be as developed, but whether volunteer or professional, the musician is nevertheless due respect from the clergyperson, of the kind that says, "We are colleagues in this process." The way clergy and musician work together is the key to the "success" of music in worship:

> A musician has skills, just as I have skills, to exercise ministry. Even though the rules of the church may say that I have the final authority in matters regarding music, that [authority] really has no power in and of itself. The real power comes in how the two of us work together.

He equates the dedication of the musician and that of the clergy, each to his own vocation. "So they are deserving of every bit of respect that I can give to them, just as I'm deserving of their respect."

Music Leadership in the Life of the Congregation

The dean believes musical leadership is critical to the life of any congregation because music is tied so closely to worship. He understands worship as the core of Christian community and believes music is critical to the vitality of that core. "If worship is empowered, then the whole rest of the life of the community will be empowered and enriched." The life of the community might include fellowship hours, Sunday school, Bible study, retreats, the mission work of the church in the community, and the telling of "my faith" stories to help others recognize their own stories. But none of this community life is possible unless it is empowered by worship, where music is a powerful ally. Because music is so integral to worship, it is also integral to the core of who we are. He observes that other organizations do a good job of forming people to be good citizens who can serve the community but adds: "I think there's a great difference between the church and a service club. The core for the church is worshiping: giving praise to Almighty God, giving thanks for the Incarnation, and trying to live 'incarnationally' in the world."

The choir school has brought responsibilities for leadership that might not be found elsewhere for those holding church-music positions. The interactions between the choir school and the congregation have brought interesting dynamics to the church. The musician explains, "Even though this church has had children singing in church for over a century, having neighborhood kids with the amount of diversity we now have in the choir school was an adjustment for some people." So the staff and the congregation considered how Christian education could take many different forms. One way to bridge the gaps in understanding was to link new choir families with parishioners who had been members for some time. The linked families sat together in worship in September, stayed together through coffee hour, and the longer-term members introduced the new families to other people. Everyone got to know one another. The new dynamics are changing the life of the congregation.

ABOUT THE CONGREGATION

The congregation has seemed to be even more engaged in the life of the church with the new energy of the choir school. As members define a future for their congregation, music is a big part of that new life. Theirs is a singing church, supported by an acoustic space that encourages singing, leaders who provide for it, and a community that cherishes it. This dynamic is led by a priest who defines the relationship:

> The congregation and I have respect for one another and a mutual desire for the cathedral to live out its commitment as both a worshiping and a missionary community. The congregation and the clergy leadership over the years have considered liturgy to truly be "the work of the people," and have applied their resources and their energy to using liturgy as a vehicle for worship.

The choir school was established 126 years ago as an essential component of the cathedral. Singing is considered the voice of worship, and a missionary/evangelistic "tool" for serving the world and inviting others into fellowship.

Financial resources have followed the commitment to be a worshiping community. The priest says high-quality music is important to the congregation because members want to offer the best to the Lord both for their own formation and for the world where they live. Whenever resources have been needed to fulfill these goals, monetary or otherwise, the congregation has found the means to provide them.

Vatican II Ideals at Work

Episcopal choirs sometimes offer choral settings of the eucharistic liturgy on behalf of the congregation. Many beautiful settings can be found in the Anglican repertoire, and, indeed, it could be argued that active listening of the congregation is full participation. In this setting however, the "full, active, and conscious participation of the people" means that the responsorial parts of the liturgy are sung by the congregation. At every point where the congregation is to sing, the people's participation is immediate and fully involved.

The dean is committed to the ideals of full participation and music as integral to the liturgy. He believes music is part of who we are as human beings and that music is essential to the community gathered for worship. He says, "Aspects of the hymns and the anthems may be teaching or informative. Some are uplifting, inspiring, engaging. But everything we do with liturgy—and music is an integral part of it—should be done with a sense of how it is encouraging and supporting the gathering community."

The Music Program

The music program is central to the life of the cathedral these days as the focal point for the renewal of the life of the congregation. The congregation seeks to build on the traditions of its past, investing similarly but with new emphases, in an area that has always been deeply rooted in the lives and faith of the community.

RESOURCES

The dean sees the education and background of the staff as resources for liturgy. For example, in his prior appointment, the organist/choirmaster had grown up in England, one associate was keenly interested in liturgy, the bishop's field in seminary had been liturgy, and the dean himself was actively involved in the liturgical renewal movement. The energy and interest of the people with their varied backgrounds were the greatest resources. Here, similarly, it is the musicians of the choir school and the clergy who most profoundly affect worship.

The lectionary is another major resource for worship. At this cathedral, the Revised Common Lectionary is used, and the Gospel is often the basis for the homily. The musician begins with the lectionary in selecting the music, first reading the Scriptures and then turning to *The Hymnal 1982, Lift Every Voice and Sing II,* and *A Scriptural Index to the Hymnal 1982.*

Instruments are further resources for worship. There are two organs in the sanctuary, along with a fine Steinway piano and a harpsichord. A portative organ resides in the chapel but can easily be moved into the sanctuary. The organs receive maintenance twice a year, with other occasional tunings. The piano is tuned regularly.

As to the space itself, the musician cites the musical challenges—the long, narrow chancel with an arch at the nave, ceiling tiles, and hollow walls. For concert performance, the choir stands on the altar steps to create a tiered effect. When the choir is positioned outside the arch and stands in the nave, its sound carries nicely. So although the acoustics of the chancel are not ideal, the sound in the nave itself is acoustically live and encourages singing. The congregation does have detailed plans for acoustical renovations of the chancel area, including replacement of ceiling tiles with a harder surface to create even better acoustics for singing.

The dean believes the space of this cathedral invites good classical Anglican/Episcopal music and confesses that this is the music that "fills [his] heart." He also recognizes the changing demographics that invite alternative music, such as the African piece sung the previous Sunday. He thinks the critical thing is to do the music well.

The choir school is paying about half the musician's salary. The earnings from an endowment pay for maintenance of the organs. Approximately $25,000 covers section leaders' salaries and other music expenses.

About the Choir School

The current incarnation of the choir school builds on the English tradition of boys' choir schools in cathedrals; a school has been here since the late nineteenth century. Now, however, the choir school includes both boys and girls, who participate in liturgy with an adult choir of both men and women. The choir school children range in age from seven to seventeen and are trained to sing at a professional level. Fifty percent of the choristers live in lower-income neighborhoods and could not afford to attend the after-school program if it were not for the $3,000-per-child scholarship program. Other parents drive from miles away and pay full tuition so their children can experience the music education offered in the program.

The curriculum consists of private lessons, mentoring, leadership formation, choir rehearsals, and participation in performances and cathedral liturgies. Children without access to pianos are given electronic keyboards to take home for piano practice. All children are matched with adult mentors who help them develop academic and life skills beyond the musical education available in the choir school. The children are involved in choir-school programming approximately seven to ten hours per week during the school year.

A full-time fund development person is employed to write grants, solicit donations, organize fundraising activities, help with marketing, and build an endowment that eventually will fund the choir school. The program has received numerous grants and awards, including some prestigious national recognition, and has built a solid alumni and donor constituency of supporters over its decade of existence.

The choir school has given new energy and direction to the cathedral. It builds on earlier traditions, offers children a high-quality musical and educational experience, involves gifted children in the immediate neighborhood as well as others from afar, energizes the liturgical life of the cathedral, and brings new parishioners into the community of faith.

The new program is not without its challenges, of course. The congregation has not always been as diverse as the neighborhood. The children in the choir school, for the most part, were not baptized in the church. As the dean says, "These kids are not all Episcopalians. We don't bring them in here saying, 'We're going to indoctrinate you.' But, since they are so integrally involved with liturgy, it would be an ideal time to help them understand what is happening." Another challenge is to balance the two missions of the school and the cathedral, which have their separate demands but also overlap in function and administration.

Tradition that Begets New Tradition

Perhaps the most exciting part of being at the cathedral these days is watching the old traditions come alive again in the revival of the cathedral through the choir school. The dean says, "This cathedral is in the great Anglican tradition and does it well. I think the biggest difference from other places is the choir school and the gift it gives."

He says the children and young people are inspiring to watch as they lead worship. The congregants experience great joy as the children become part of their lives. Worshipers get to watch the children develop over the course of a church year. An additional benefit to the cathedral is that the choir brings new people into the life of the congregation. A number of families who were not members have come because their children are part of the choir school. While the choir children are in rehearsal from 9:00 to 10:00 on Sunday mornings, the families participate in programs for adults and siblings, and then they stay for worship.

The musician appreciates the cohesiveness of the cathedral congregation and the absence of factions or power struggles even during this time of transition. He has felt the unifying power of the vision for both maintaining the tradition of high-quality music and building on that foundation to encompass a diversity the members had not considered before. For example, the lections for the Sunday of the site visit included Jesus's command to let go of all material wealth and follow him. The musician chose the *Magnificat,* with the text "He sent the rich away empty," and used a musical setting based on Latin American rhythms by Brian Kelly. For communion the children sang "Siyahamba," or "We are marching in the light of God," the South African freedom song that many of the choristers could readily identify with. Yet the first hymn, "O God, Our Help in Ages Past," was sung to the traditional tune ST. ANNE, and the organ prelude was J. S. Bach's St. Anne Fugue. So "tradition" here is based on the long Anglican history that spans many historical musical periods, including contemporary music, a tradition that is continually renewed when high standards for music selection are upheld. The music comes from a wealth of repertoire that serves the Scriptures for the day. Much choral music in the Anglican tradition is composed to fit the lections, so a repertoire is readily available, and that repertoire expands as Anglican musicians write new hymns and anthems.

LITURGICAL PIETIES

The commitments this congregation makes to its worship and its quality of music are based both in the Episcopal Church itself and in the congregants' historic practice of their faith in this place. The dean reflects first on the contributions of Anglicans to worship and then talks about the way these contributions are expressed at this cathedral:

We're a people of liturgy, rather than emphasizing theology and preaching as other denominations might. Our focal point is our worship—*The Book of Common Prayer*. You want to know about us—what we believe? The best place to go is the *The Book of Common Prayer*. So I think the great gift we give, at least to Western Christendom, is Sunday by Sunday, doing liturgy well.

He believes one liturgical piety at the cathedral could be described by the kinds of diversity that have developed in the last ten or fifteen years, namely, diversity in age (ranging from tiny ones in the choir to old-timers in the congregation), gender (many adult males attend), race, and sexual orientation. Then there is the diversity of religious experience, from longtime members of the congregation, some of whom entered the cathedral's worshiping life as far back as 1928, to people who have just started coming in the past year. They may have come from Presbyterian, Catholic, or even Baptist or Pentecostal backgrounds. Outward expressions of piety range from those who genuflect when entering the pew to those who talk before the liturgy begins, and those who cross themselves during liturgy while others don't know what the gesture means. Yet the liturgy itself and the music that the congregation participates in so joyfully are the unifying elements amid this diversity.

A TIME WHEN THINGS WENT WRONG

The dean values the good congregational singing at the cathedral and does not take the leadership of the people's song for granted. He recounts a time early in his ministry when he needed to fill the organist/choir director position in the parish he was serving. A retired organist was recommended whom the parish could afford. However, on the first Sunday, the choir seemed unsettled before the service. The prelude went well, but when it came time for the congregation to sing, it was clear that the organist's hymn-playing was not adequately supporting the singing. The priest shared his concern, but the organist did not seem to understand. The same thing happened the following Sunday. This time, when the priest met with him, the organist said he could not work with the priest, and resigned. The priest learned early on that not all organists, even good ones, appreciate the importance of congregational singing. He has considered leading congregational song a primary skill in hiring an organist ever since.

He says that almost every Sunday, something happens that you hadn't "put into the works" and that you just have to go on. Wrong numbers for hymns have been printed, or the psalm has not been printed, so the congregation cannot respond, for example. "So, at that point, I just stop and say, 'Folks, we need to regroup here. Let's all get on the same page.'" Or occasionally the organist will lose his place in the music, ending the hymn after four verses when it has five. The priest may just smile and acknowledge the omission, allowing everyone to move on without focusing on the slip-up.

The musician recalls a prior position he held, where divisions in the congregation made leading the music program difficult. He is grateful for the current environment that is more cohesive in spirit and vision.

The Old Begets the New

This is a traditional Episcopal cathedral church with a rich history of good music and liturgy. The congregation takes seriously its responsibility to continue that tradition.

The cathedral finds itself in an environment very different from that of fifty years ago. It is responding creatively and in dialogue with the people of the neighborhood to provide a resource to enrich the lives of the children and families through music and liturgy. Through the innovative choir school, the members are building on their tradition, remaining faithful to the integrity of that tradition, adapting to their new circumstances, and serving the community where the cathedral is located. The congregation has a new life, purpose, and calling to fulfill.

HEAR

CHAPTER 7

Vital Music in Worship
Shapes Life and Service

THIS LIVELY CONGREGATION WAS BEGUN BY SIX FAMI-
lies in 1862 as a Cumberland Presbyterian church, joining
Methodist and Baptist congregations in a frontier town. In the
early twentieth century it became part of a northern predeces-
sor body of the 1983 reunion of two streams of Presbyterianism
that formed the Presbyterian Church (U.S.A.). The congregation now numbers about 750. The current sanctuary was built
in 1942, a rectangular space that then not only provided for the
sanctuary but also was used for Sunday school, as the fellowship
hall, and as a USO center during World War II. Older members
of the congregation remember that during worship they could
smell chicken cooking in the fellowship hall (now the balcony of
the sanctuary). At the back of the current sanctuary and under
the former fellowship hall were the Sunday school classrooms.
Two spaces on either side of the chancel area, which once served
as church offices, now house the chambers for the pipe organ.
The long rectangular nave is framed by wooden beams and
is focused on the intimate chancel area with its central cross,
organ pipes, and choir seating, which is perpendicular to the
congregation. The focal point is the cross, indicating that the
reason for gathering is to worship God.

The congregation has embraced the presence of the regional university in the town, which has grown significantly in the past two decades. For more than fifty years, the church has sponsored a scholarship program for university music students who sing in the choir and become part of the church family. The students are often "adopted" by families in the church who remain in contact with them long after they graduate. Many go on to significant leadership positions in churches, schools, and performance venues. Former students often return to the congregation to sing in the choir, give recitals, or offer music for worship, enriching the musical life of the congregation. Members of the congregation return the favor, traveling to performances or special events of these former students.

The commitment of the congregation to significant music in worship has spanned multiple musicians and pastors. A former pastor and current member of the church recalls that the musical tradition has been strong under the leadership of at least three music directors, including the current director, who came in 1972. He firmly believes that the music tradition is owned by the congregation and only led by the current pastor and music director.

That music is important in the life of this congregation is obvious. Though the acoustics are not particularly helpful, the congregational singing is vibrant. Everyone holds a hymnal and sings. Worshipers expect the music to be a special part of worship. Conversations among worshipers after the service are often about the music of the day. The children's choirs are led by a former music educator who elicits a beautiful sound and clear diction from the children. An adult bell choir plays approximately once a month. The adult choir is small, primarily because the chancel area is small, but the singers are extremely competent and committed. Two identical services are offered on Sunday morning, and an alternative Sunday night service with informal music was being offered on a trial basis at the time of our site visit. Music is a drawing card for new members, who know they can anticipate hearing substantive music every week in worship.

The importance of high-quality music and worship is but one aspect of the vibrant life of this church. Also of note are the strong adult-education programs both on Sunday and during the week, and the church's many outreach programs. In particular, on Wednesday evenings during the academic year a full curriculum of courses is offered on a wide variety of topics, beginning with Bible study but also including parenting studies, book studies, exploration of non-Western religions, finance and stewardship classes, theology classes taught by professors from a regional seminary, and various healing ministries. A recent twelve-week hymnology class drew from twenty-five to thirty participants each week who were not otherwise involved in music programs. The church also has an unusually large number of members who have significant leadership roles in the community, including past and current mayors, city council members, chamber of commerce presidents, and leaders of nonprofit organizations. One member was chair of the school board when the city schools were integrated. Other members are leaders in the university and local businesses. An active worship life is one dimension of a multidimensional faith commitment of this body of believers. Members could not imagine it otherwise.

The Leaders

The senior pastor has served this congregation for twenty years. He manages the professional staff, including another pastor, a director of Christian education, and the music director. He also preaches, teaches, provides pastoral care, and takes particular interest in planning for worship. He especially enjoys choosing hymns to accompany the theological themes for the day. He often serves as cantor for the psalm of the day. He is particularly well suited to these tasks because of his background, formation, and interests. He studied piano and organ during his elementary and high school years with a Catholic nun who insisted that he master a basic repertoire of classical music, providing a standard he now appreciates. "That was the only thing that my teacher would teach. If you wanted something else, you went somewhere else." The musicians of the Presbyterian church his family attended gave him opportunity to use his music skills. He recalls that this small church did not have many resources and often struggled to do music well. But he remembers the music director saying, "We may not be able to do what a large choir does, but we are going to do decent music." He says that made a big impression on him. He sang in the church choir, played organ for some services at his own church and others, and was the organist for chapel services while attending seminary. His voice study and participation in high-school musicals prepared him for the community musicals he now is part of, a way of extending his ministry beyond the church.

Although the pastor was raised Presbyterian, he never considered a vocation in the church until after college and a short stint in the Army. While pursuing a career in professional theater, he auditioned and earned a slot in the choir at Madison Avenue Presbyterian Church in New York City. The dynamic preaching he heard while singing in that choir began to change his mind about such a profession. A sense of call to the ministry developed out of that context.

The musician's title is minister of music, one he inherited, appreciates, and wants to keep. He is employed full time at the university, and in this part-time position at the church he directs the chancel (adult) choir and has charge of the music program, spending most of his time with worship planning and administration. He oversees the organist, the director of two children's choirs, and the adult volunteer director of a handbell choir. Part of his job is to coordinate the quartet of student soloists who serve as section leaders for the choir. These university students, who are part of a scholarship program, also sing at the 8:30 a.m. service. He chooses music for them to sing in the first service in lieu of a choir anthem, coordinating the choices with the rest of the service. He also serves as mentor for the students and liaison between the students and the congregation.

The parents of the minister of music were amateur musicians; his father played the piano, and his mother was a singer. They spent a lot of time at their church, a large and musically sophisticated Baptist congregation where he learned a lot about church music. The cathedral-like church building was built when he was seven years old. He remembers seeing the beautiful stained-glass windows, hearing the choir, and thinking, "Wow. That's the most beautiful thing I've ever heard." The organ was an important part of the music program, and the organist was his piano teacher. He considers the minister of music in that church as one of the great influences in his life. He began to study violin, his principal instrument, at age eight, and later studied piano, organ, and trombone. But it was the minister of music at the church who made sure that he was in the children's choir, played organ for Bible school, held notes for the organ tuner, and conducted Mozart's *Ave Verum Corpus* at age fourteen. He says of his mentor, "He was a great Christian leader—sincere, hardworking, a very good musician, and a great example. He didn't talk about what was important to do. He just did it." The musician feels very much a part of the church, even though he is an employee. "My kids grew up here. They were baptized here. They were married here. This is our home church."

VIEWS OF MUSIC IN LITURGY

The pastor sees music as central to the liturgy and chooses the hymns carefully to fit the Scriptures for the day. He takes special care that the hymn following the sermon is paired with the biblical text on which the sermon is based, and with the theme of the sermon. The music then reinforces the preacher's words. He explains, "I see music not as an add-on, but as a means of carrying the gospel message, bearing witness to the good news not in a superficial or tacked-on way but right at the core of the liturgy."

He is pleased that the liturgical renewal of the past few years has brought back the singing of psalms in the Presbyterian church. He believes psalms are vital to congregational singing and worship, and he is grateful for the large section of *The Presbyterian Hymnal* devoted to psalm settings. An unusual aspect of psalm-singing in this church is that the pastor often serves as cantor for the psalm, which he did on the Sunday that was part of this study. The effectiveness of his service as cantor rested not only on his clear singing voice, but also on the importance he gave to the text. The pastor approached the task first as a communicator of text and then as a musician to deliver that text effectively. The proclamation of the text was made more beautiful by the music, but the "performance" of the music never got in the way of the text.

Worthy of note is the coherence achieved by the worship planners. The worship service was on the Sunday before Thanksgiving, which was also Christ the King Sunday, a day that required a bit of finessing to meet both liturgical and seasonal needs. While using the lections for the day and choosing "Crown Him with Many Crowns" and "All Hail the Power of Jesus' Name!" as the opening and closing hymns, the worship planners also acknowledged Thanksgiving. The choir anthem by Joel Martinson addressed both themes: "O Praise Ye the Lord!" mentions praising God "in the height" and also that "Thanksgiving and song to him be outpoured all ages along!" The hymn "Come, Ye Thankful People, Come" was sung before the presentation of tithes and offerings. The organ prelude and postlude bookended the service with music appropriate to Christ the King. A coherent service resulted.

The minister of music believes there should be a clear reason for any piece of music to be included in the worship service. It should relate to a reading in the lectionary, for example, or it should otherwise emphasize the spoken word. He thinks that music can express the same theology as the spoken word. If the words are set to music, the variety allows a new hearing of the text, giving it greater meaning. This musician and the pastor work together toward integrated worship, sometimes without even conferring, because they know each other well after working together for so many years. The pastor thinks musically, and the musician thinks textually. The result is a coherent whole.

Asked to identify the ultimate outcome they seek, the pastor says, "For the people to have an experience of God, that they are in God's presence, that God's love is dominant." He thinks this happens if an experience of transcendence results. He thinks much worship today is plagued by a lack of transcendence, coming off as informal. The result is that worshipers miss the "bigness" and glory of God.

What Makes for a Good Leader?

The pastor identifies a good leader as someone who is conscientious about his or her job, dependable, and a self-starter. He enjoys working with leaders who "take the bull by the horns and go with it." He then defines leadership using a concept he calls "old-fashioned churchmanship." A "churchman" is

> someone who constantly has the best interest of the church at heart. [Churchmanship] is a combination of qualities—showing up, being willing to take on tasks that affect the greater good, dependability. It means having an interest in the church for the sake of the gospel, not necessarily for what I or my family is going to get out of it. It is a way of looking at the life of the church through the lens of the gospel, which always asks of us some kind of sacrifice for the sake of the greater good.

The musician believes that leading by example is best. He tries to do that by preparing, being flexible, being creative—whatever is needed. That may mean picking up the choir robes off the floor or carrying instruments up and down the stairs. Others follow his example. He notes that such service does not feel burdensome, because the congregation is appreciative.

Can appreciation be expressed by applause during a worship service? The musician thinks applause is almost an insult in that it cheapens the offering by focusing the attention on those making it. He sees applause as an interruption, similar to an announcement inserted in the middle of the service. ("The only announcement you really need is, 'There's a fire in the building.'")

The Role of the Professional Musician

The pastor values competence and a solid musical education in a church musician. He defines competence as having a repertoire of solid, classical church music, along with a willingness to use a diverse music repertoire so that the faith can be expressed in many ways. Because of the centrality of music in worship, the music leaders need to be top-notch. If they are not, the quality of the liturgy suffers. As an example of the commitment he seeks, he cites the professional organist at the church who has a full-time position at a university in another community and drives several hours one way each weekend to play at the church. She has done this for ten years. The congregation has made a commitment to high-quality musical leadership, and the musical leaders respond with equal commitment.

The musician describes his job as setting the expectations for other musicians and then helping them meet them. He first needs to know how to set high standards and then where to find the resources the musicians need to meet those standards. Balancing musical standards and pastoral sensibilities can be tricky, especially for young college students, who may not understand how seriously this congregation takes its responsibility for good music and that this is not the typical church music job. Sometimes direct, straightforward instruction is necessary, such as, "If you are going to sing that piece, it had better be good." Yet sometimes that approach can backfire. One student said, "Every time I get up to sing here, I'm so in awe of all of the people that I've heard about who sang here before, and how wonderful they were and are. It just makes me so nervous, I can't even sing." So the music director tries not to make the experience quite so hard on them.

The music director also finds himself using his experience as an organist, brass player, and violinist. For example, when the organist needs time to turn the page or change a piston, the music director knows to allow the organist time or to listen for the "thunk" of the piston changing. He knows brass players need to breathe, and that they have an understanding of rhythm and cut-offs different from that of choral singers. He knows string bowings and can say, "There's a down-bow there," often surprising the players. His variety of skills makes for ease in rehearsal and finesse in the final musical product, enabling the other professional musicians to give their best.

Musical Leadership in the Life of the Congregation

The pastor has a friend who says that the hymnal may be the most important book in the church in that the people learn as much about theology and the gospel from the hymns as from the Bible. He hastens to add that most good hymns are rooted in the biblical message, and that this idea is not a matter of "either/or" but "both/and." His understanding of the importance of hymns underlies the care with which he chooses hymns— because they relate to the Scriptures and sermon for the day, rather than because they are familiar or well liked. The pastor believes a music leader who understands the "crucial conduit between the gospel and the congregation" is essential to good music leadership and is grateful to work with a musician who shares that understanding.

The pastor notes that members of the congregation mention the music almost every Sunday; he believes that the music has helped individuals in a particular service feel "closer to God." He connects this regular occurrence to the fact that the music director and organist go to great lengths to make it known that they are not performing. God, not those in the pew, is the audience for all music that is offered—a critical distinction. It may seem odd to some that this pastor is as pleased to hear comments about the music as he might be to hear compliments on a sermon. He does not distinguish between the two. The goal is to provide the people a way to worship authentically.

The musician is grateful that his thirty-eight years of service to the congregation have enabled him to learn what hymn or anthem is meaningful to an individual or family. This information is especially helpful in planning weddings and funerals. His length of tenure also helps him understand what meaning special services or traditions marking points in the life of the congregation have for the members. For instance, "God Be with You Till We Meet Again" is sung by the congregation whenever someone in the choir is leaving. No one knows who started the tradition; it had already begun when he was a student at the university. If you attend the church for a while, you know what the singing of that hymn means.

The musician also believes that the Presbyterian order of worship can have a ministry of its own. He cites as an example one of the scholarship students who had attended church all his life but not in a congregation where liturgy was valued. This student found over time that the structure of the service itself became meaningful. He discovered that the progression of the liturgy allowed him to worship in new and deeper ways.

FULL, CONSCIOUS, AND ACTIVE PARTICIPATION

The pastor believes wholeheartedly that music is a necessary, integral part of the liturgy. He sees music as a "vessel and instrument" for the gospel. When music is offered well and without self-consciousness, it is a natural part of the proclamation of the Word and becomes a beautiful, consequential act.

This congregation uses the Service for the Lord's Day from *The Book of Common Worship* with its responsorial liturgy that the pastor believes has encouraged active participation of the people. In particular, the congregation naturally responds to "The Word of the Lord" after a Scripture reading by saying "Thanks be to God," whether or not it is printed in the bulletin. The congregation participates fully in the singing in the service, which always includes at least three hymns. Some hymns are familiar, but one is usually less well known, yet all are chosen with the understanding that the primary choir is the congregation. The chancel choir is considered the auxiliary choir, whose role is to enable the people to "make a joyful noise unto the Lord."

The pastor is a bit wistful about the opportunity for congregational participation in the Episcopal liturgy; he wishes his Presbyterian congregation could respond with "Amen" as frequently as Episcopalians do. The response, meaning "So be it," reflects corporate ownership of the prayer that has been spoken. It is prescribed in the Episcopal liturgy but not in the Presbyterian liturgy.

The musician thinks the Vatican II documents are simply about Roman Catholics "turning Protestant," in that Protestants have always valued the participation of the people, particularly in the singing of hymns and psalms. For Protestants, music is so integral to the liturgy that it does not even have to be mentioned: "We just do it."

Structuring and Sustaining the Music Program

The pastor says his primary resources for substantive worship are the music director, the four paid soloists, and his clergy colleagues. He understands the financial commitment the church makes to pay these professionals and appreciates it. He also understands the value that the arts programs in the community and the university give in their capacity to nurture the musical staff and to participate in musical events at the church from time to time. He and his wife were able to take a Lilly Endowment–funded sabbatical during which he attended artistic events and religious services in Great Britain that were sources of inspiration.

The operations budget provides approximately $3,800 yearly for print music, instrumentalists, and piano maintenance. The music director and organist are salaried, with an additional $2,100 allowed for substitute organists. The four paid scholarship students are paid from a $23,470 line item. In addition, gifts of as much as two to three thousand dollars at Christmas and Easter provide money for anthems and extra instrumentalists. The organ is considered part of the building for insurance purposes and is maintained from the buildings and grounds budget.

The church has an endowment fund for organ recitals that has not been used for several years because the organ needs major repairs. A committee will establish a budget for these repairs and seek funding to pay for them, probably in the range of several hundred thousand dollars. A foundation that helped with the purchase of the organ is a likely source for funding. The congregation is eager to complete the work so that recitals and hymn festivals can resume.

The music program falls under the purview of the congregation's worship and music committee, but this group does not offer major input on week-to-week decisions. The committee organizes ushers, makes arrangements for communion, provides for flowers, and schedules readers, for example, while the clergy and music staff make the weekly music and liturgy decisions. When major changes are being considered, however, the committee is consulted, and "we discuss it intently," says the music minister. As to the service itself, it is understood by the committee and professional staff that the liturgy comes from *The Book of Common Worship* and that the Scriptures for the day are from the Revised Common Lectionary.

Nature of the Program

The children's choirs are directed by a now-retired music-education teacher who began employment at the church at the same time as the music director. She was also a soloist in the choir in the 1960s. To watch and hear the children sing is a joy. They display discipline; rehearse once a week after school; sing with understanding of text and music, which have been chosen with care; shape vowels beautifully; sound their consonants; and sing from memory with full but not forced tone. The children attend a regional music conference with the director for a week every summer. Sustaining a youth choir has been difficult, and there is no such choir at present. When the church had an active youth choir, it was directed by a university student.

The adult choir rehearses on both Wednesday night and Sunday morning to accommodate members who cannot come during the week or who may want to attend Sunday school. The music director organizes the rehearsal schedule so that everything is practiced several weeks ahead, allowing time for choir members to feel confident about the music by the time they sing it in a service. The director is careful to keep the rehearsal within the allotted time.

The organist is insistent that she not choose her music until she knows what the hymns and other music for the day will be. This decision often means that she must work quickly so that titles and composers can be inserted in the worship bulletin before printing.

Musical Traditions

The pastor says the music used by the congregation is good, solid church music, "not fluff, but 'classical' in the best sense of that word." He says the congregation has a huge commitment to excellence and that the music program has support from a large segment of the membership. The scholarship program, begun in the 1940s, was very forward-thinking at the time and has continued without interruption. The music scholars provide the foundation for much of the music-making of the church. The congregation believes it is the members' responsibility to nurture these students while they are at the church and to continue the relationships after they leave. The music careers of the students are a source of pride for the members.

Many people in the congregation were not born into Presbyterian families. While music from all historic periods, including recently written music, is appreciated, more informal music is not used during the morning worship services. The children might sing music that is a bit more informal than what the adults sing. Regardless of their own musical preferences, the members expect dignity in their worship, an absence of unneeded flourish, and a humility about the musical offerings.

ROADBLOCKS TO EFFECTIVE MUSIC LEADERSHIP

The pastor cites a concern in the broader church about adopting "contemporary" or "alternative" worship. The associate pastor has taken the lead in beginning a contemporary service on Sunday evenings and has included some music that would not be used on Sunday morning. Yet that music is carefully selected to fit the liturgy, which includes many of the same elements as a Sunday morning service. One of the senior pastor's concerns is that alternative worship is not rooted in liturgical tradition, an issue the staff is trying to address in the new Sunday evening service. He would like to think that it is possible to use different kinds of music in alternative worship and to do that in the context of a liturgical service. His broader concern is that much worship today uses a "shoot-from-the-hip" approach and loses the depth and substance that the liturgy offers.

Attendance at the Sunday evening service ranges from thirty to fifty people, a small group in comparison to the morning services. Some people who have attended in the morning come back in the evening to support the new effort. A diverse group of musicians who play various instruments take seriously their role in the service, rehearsing every Tuesday evening. At this writing, the effort is still considered an experiment.

Asked about roadblocks to effective leadership, the musician admits he sometimes thinks *he* is the roadblock. He finds it hard to focus on the job when he knows of grudges or personnel problems or when there are distractions in worship. He acknowledges that it is hard for him to ignore minor annoyances and keep on track to help the minister and congregation with their worship. A few times budgetary cuts have made it difficult to maintain the quality of the program and have required difficult choices. But perhaps a more significant difficulty is managing the balance between a full-time job outside the church and a part-time job at the church. He jokes that people should give more notice when they intend to die. At times, he has to spend considerable time arranging for a funeral service but cannot take time off from work to attend the service. And sometimes his family gets peeved with him for giving in to his pastoral inclinations. For example, one Christmas Day, after he had been up late directing music for Christmas Eve services, a bride wanted to talk with him about her wedding music while she was in town. His adult son said, "Dad, why don't you tell her to leave you alone? Aren't you going to have Christmas?"

Leadership in the Congregation

The pastor believes his leadership is enabled by a congregation that respects and trusts him. His ministry of twenty years in this place has allowed a mutual relationship to develop that creates all kinds of possibilities for him as a leader and for the congregation. The congregation and pastor know and love each other. The pastor does not like experimentation and does not throw surprises at the congregation—a good fit for this particular church. The pastor wants the parishioners to become who they are, to be the best they can be. And the way this congregation worships is part of who they are. The music of their worship grows out of their environment and feeds it. They are willing to put resources into the music program because they know it is important to them as a congregation, and it nourishes them. They want to make sure the program is maintained at a level of excellence. The pastor understands this dynamic and helps to lead members into a deeper understanding of their liturgy and music of worship. He helps to feed them intellectually, spiritually, emotionally, and musically. It is part of his understanding of leadership to guide them but not to dictate who they must be.

The musician thinks the congregation has developed a tradition of formal worship over many years. It is who these people are, so they appreciate and encourage it, and people come to the church because of it. The church has been on the same downtown corner for 150 years. The members have called leaders who have supported and grown that vision with them.

Asked how the Sunday night service fits into the strong ethos of formal worship, the musician says it doesn't. He sometimes thinks the service is being done because some members in the church want an outlet for their music-making. He went to great lengths to find someone to lead the music for that service when it first began. His bottom line is that whatever is done should be good. Though many churches with a strong formal music program would not consider such an experiment, this church is confident enough in its identity to try a new way of worshiping.

The musician thinks it is rather remarkable that the congregation sings so well in an acoustically dead room. He says worshipers sing first because of their willingness to sing. Second, the leaders make great effort to choose hymns the congregation knows and to prepare the people to sing hymns they do not know. The pastor and the musician choose hymns that obviously relate to the themes of the service. Music not in the hymnal is printed in the bulletin so that music readers can lead from the congregation. Finally, the organist is capable in leading the congregational singing. The music director is grateful to have an organist with that ability.

Asked why the church puts money and other resources into high-quality worship and music leadership, the musician said he believes it is in part the congregation's commitment to education. Members want the best educational experiences for their children and high-quality intellectual discussions in educational classes in the church. The professional staff sets the standard. Members also expect music that is worthy of use in worship—music of integrity. They are outspoken about their support, saying, "If we have to cut something, we don't want to cut music."

Summary

This congregation is both mature and vibrant, with deep roots in a community and its traditions, yet in constant communication with the present. These are a people of wisdom who value the past, engage the present, and look to the future with hope and optimism. They take their commitments to music seriously, because they take their faith seriously and value education and intellectual substance. Music is an important vehicle for expression of their Christian faith and a means by which that faith is nourished. Their music is remarkable and transcendent, as is their worship, and that is precisely what they expect it to be.

STAND FAST

CHAPTER 8

Music Keeps Heart,
Mind, and Mission in Sync

THE CHURCH WAS FOUNDED IN 1949 IN A MOSTLY UNDE-
veloped part of a large southwestern city. The growth of the city
in the late twentieth century was mirrored by the growth of the
church, as its location became an urban residential neighborhood, strategically located and accessible to parishioners from
many directions. Music has always been an important part of
the church, with a succession of fine musicians building an
increasingly broad and deep music program. Former pastors and
musicians have remained in contact with the church, returning
in informal and professional capacities from time to time.

The church has about 2,850 members, with 12 to 14 percent
of the congregation directly involved in the music program. The
music staff includes a full-time music director, an organist, and
a children's choir/handbell director, as well as seven part-time
paid section leaders in the adult choir. But the range of music
in the program is made possible by the many professional musicians who volunteer as choir members or soloists because they
have chosen to attend this church. Several part-time volunteer
music librarians contribute many hours of work each week.

Within the past decade, the church decided to renovate its
sanctuary and to provide new facilities for the music program.
The music staff members were told to make a list of everything

they might want, and as one of the music staff says, "We pretty much got everything." The church invested in new rehearsal facilities, a new organ in the sanctuary, new offices for music staff, new storage facilities, and a complete remodeling of the sanctuary that took into consideration acoustics for both speaking and music. The rectangular worship space has transepts and a rear balcony with an organ, and the chancel has a choir loft and organ in the front. The walls are white with translucent windows, classical pillars, and dental moldings. A large brass Celtic cross hangs above the communion table.

Three nearly identical Sunday morning services are offered, an early one in the chapel with soloist and organ, and two services in the sanctuary with one or more choirs. Additional services are scheduled during Advent, Lent, and Holy Week, and the adult choir performs a special evening concert in the fall and spring as well as one patriotic concert each year. A children's musical is given each summer, and the youth put on a musical every two years.

Teamwork within Hierarchy

Music and worship decisions are made by the senior pastor, the music director, and the organist as a team, but the hierarchy is clear: The senior pastor says, "I'm head of staff, which means that I'm responsible for the overall supervision and oversight of staff." His major responsibilities include preaching and leading worship, providing pastoral care, and overseeing the bigger picture. He supervises the director of music, who supervises the rest of the music staff. Further, he sees his role as one of support for the music staff, providing resources for their programs so they can function without interruption.

The music director conducts the adult choir, and until recently, also led the youth choir. He oversees the rest of the music program, which includes three children's choirs from preschool through sixth grade, three handbell choirs, and the youth choir. He also coordinates the weekly bulletin. Though his job description does not require him to do so, he regularly makes hospital visits to choir members and their families and to music staff. The organist provides music for all services and accompanies rehearsals. The next responsibility listed on the job description is "practice," and she is glad that "the church feels that it is important to prepare." She also works with hymn selection, meeting with the pastor and music director a week and a half before the service to choose the hymns to fit the liturgy and the lectionary preaching plan. She also is responsible for the music for the soloist at the early service and for the psalm setting the cantor leads. She is the primary contact for music for weddings and provides music for funerals and memorial services.

A third music staff member directs one children's and one adult handbell choir, and one of the graded children's choirs, and supervises two other children's choirs. She plans the music and spiritual-formation curriculum for all the children's music groups and directs a creative-arts workshop for children in the summer. Though not a part of the weekly planning meetings, she works with the music director in scheduling the children's and handbell choirs in worship.

Musical Formation

The pastor was always interested in music as a child. He sang in church and school choirs and played in concert and marching bands in high school and college, including first-chair tuba in the Intercollegiate Concert Band. During college he also sang in the concert choir. His parents were musical, both singing in the church choir. They lived in a small college town and went to all the concerts on campus. His father, an elder in the church, enjoyed choral concerts, but the pastor remembers that his father was always asking, "They're not going to sing anything by Charles Ives, are they?" He believes music was a very important part of his early years.

The music director's earliest memory is "sitting on the piano bench next to my mom while she was playing for church. My mom was a piano teacher, and my dad was a cowboy and horse trainer. I think the music part stuck, though." He sang in children's choir at church starting at about fourth grade and was in the band program at school. His high school didn't have a choir until his senior year. He had planned to become a high school band director, but in his junior year at university, a new choral conductor arrived. He became so excited about choral music that he changed his focus and after graduation worked as a senior-high choral director for six years. Even in high school, he had a sense of calling to go into church work. After five or six years in teaching, he experienced a "spiritual renewal and felt a sense of calling." He explains, "I was working part time in a church, and they put me on full time, doing youth ministries and music ministry. They were really supportive. They sent me to seminary, paid all my expenses."

The organist cannot remember when she *wasn't* interested in music. Her mother and father both sang in choirs in the little church where she grew up, and her father directed the male chorus. Her mother made sure that all four children had piano lessons. She played for Sunday school classes as early as fourth grade and for choirs through high school. Because there were plenty of good pianists around, she also got to sing. She was totally unaware of organ music, because for a long time the church had only a piano. When the congregation bought a little electronic organ, her mother said she should take lessons, so the church would have an organist. She took a few organ lessons from a student at the college and later from a professor who awakened her interest in the organ. She remembers, "I picked it up really quickly. He gave me difficult music right away, and it was rewarding." After college graduation and some international work, she returned to the U.S. to play part time in churches. The joy in those first jobs led her to go to graduate school in organ and to pursue work in church music.

The children's/handbell choir director was nurtured by the musician in her Presbyterian church with whom she studied piano and sang in children's choirs, and whom she assisted while in high school with the younger children's choirs. It was he who taught her to memorize and understand the meaning of hymns, instilled the love of music within her, and conveyed what it could do for her soul and how others could be served through music. Her mother always sang in the choir, while her father looked after the children whose parents were singing in the choir—the "choir orphans." After college graduation she was a performer first—a professional percussionist—and taught piano lessons while volunteering her skills at the church. She still enjoys playing professionally, but she has found her heart's vocation in the church.

FINDING A VOCATION

All these leaders talk about their paths into church work as a combination of (1) an inner, reflective journey, (2) experiences that allowed them to "try out" a vocation, and (3) relationships with people who encouraged them to consider the church as the arena of their vocation.

The pastor recalls from his childhood:

> I was writing sermons at seven. They were very short. My mother kept them in a box, and I still have them. I had a congregation of one—her name was Debbie. There was something about worship that has fascinated me as early as I can remember. I think part of it was the power of the magical moments in the pulpit that I had seen.

Undoubtedly, he was also influenced by an uncle who was a Presbyterian minister. In high school, he was moderator of the Presbyterian Westminster Fellowship, and in the summer he worked as a church camp counselor and preached sermons on Sundays. The decision to enter the ministry was not clear-cut, however. He went to college as a chemistry major, intending to become a veterinarian. But his enthusiasm for that endeavor waned:

I finally decided—after being in a Saturday 8:00 a.m. lab class and staring into a flask—that this was not it. I had a pastor that I was very close to, and he was willing to spend a lot of time with me, thinking through the call. I changed my major from chemistry to English/liberal arts and went to seminary.

Explaining how his theology of music and worship developed, the pastor says:

I sensed something was happening in worship that was almost dramatic—perhaps theatrical—about the intersection of music and the spoken word. I'm sometimes surprised at many pastors' seeming lack of an appreciation for music. I would like to see pastors, in their formative years, have a background in music, and also in theater.

The music director remembers that Sunday was "church day" for his parents. He has always been in church on Sundays. It was part of life, not really an option, but something he loved. Then came an important experience as a teenager: "When I was in high school, we had a good youth choir program at our church. The director made us see how important what we were doing was to worship, and how we were leaders in worship. This was a significant thing to be involved in." Later, he felt a sense of "calling" and considered the change from teaching to music ministry by talking with people whose wisdom he valued. When he went back to school for a Master of Sacred Music degree, a professor gave wise counsel: "He didn't push. He just kept letting me see possibilities and opened doors to help me understand what music ministry was all about. I'll always be grateful to him."

The organist finished an undergraduate degree in music education, with organ as her performing instrument. For an organist, the church is the workplace, and it was the music that drew her into the church. The sense of vocation developed later, in part through her experiencing how music affects the people of the church. She says, "I feel very privileged to offer music that has impact on people. Not many have that opportunity. It's a responsibility, too, and sometimes I feel the responsibility is sort of overwhelming."

Mentors

The pastor feels fortunate to have grown up knowing a lot of ministers. In seminary and in his early years of ministry, he became acquainted with some wonderful people he still draws upon. Some of them are no longer living, but they still influence him: "There are many times when I've faced a situation and thought intuitively, 'How would so-and-so see this?' and tried to look at something through their eyes."

The music director considers his church music colleagues and the conductor of a professional ensemble with whom he sings as his best sources of mentoring. He exchanges ideas and repertoire with his music colleagues and gains new ideas in musicianship from the professional conductor. The organist also values her peers as sources of information and enrichment for her work.

All team members mentioned the nourishment they receive from the encouragement of members of the church and from their own families and spouses.

Planning

Critical to the planning process is the pastor's regular personal retreat, during which he charts his sermons for nine to twelve months. With sermon titles and Scriptures in hand that far in advance, the musicians can select choir music, congregational hymns, and instrumental music to support the Scripture reading and sermon topic. The pastor, music director, and organist meet weekly with one goal in mind, according to the music director: "We try to tie it all together. Sometimes it fits really well. Sometimes it doesn't fit so well. And sometimes it *accidentally* works really well."

The music director is grateful for the information that allows him to do his own job well: the outline of Scripture readings and sermon titles, and a rough idea of how the pastor thinks the sermon should go. This process contrasts sharply with some prior experiences the musician has encountered:

> I've been in situations where I didn't know what the sermon or Scripture was until the week prior, and that was in a pretty large church. That pastor wasn't overly concerned if everything tied together tightly or not. The sermon was the important thing to him. Everything else was just "icing."

The planning allows adequate time for choirs to rehearse anthems, hymns, and descants that coordinate with Scriptures and the sermon; minor adjustments can be made closer to the service, and all planners work toward the same goal. And according to the music director, they enjoy their work, "It's really fun. It's a good process."

The organist talks about a congregational committee that also participates in the process:

> Worship Mission has a big role in what happens here in worship, which includes the flower committee, the ushers, the communications person, for example. The music committee is a subcommittee of the Worship Mission. The Worship Mission also has a special worship committee that is responsible for planning Ash Wednesday, Maundy Thursday, Good Friday, and Advent services—services beyond those on Sunday morning.

The organizational structure provides input from the congregation, the preparation time each planner needs, and the rehearsals required for volunteer musicians to be confident in their offerings. The structure also allows for the creativity of the leaders and enough space to make changes when last-minute needs arise.

The Place of Music in Presbyterian Liturgy

Each member of the team brings a different perspective to his or her understanding of the place of music in worship. Their backgrounds differ: the pastor was raised in a Presbyterian church, the music director in a Baptist church, and the organist in a Mennonite church. Both musicians have graduate degrees in church music from a United Methodist institution. So it falls to the pastor to interpret the Presbyterian slant on music in liturgy, while the musicians bring the richness of other Protestant traditions and their finely honed music skills to the task.

The pastor likens music in the mainline church to "speaking in tongues," a potent ecstatic experience. He believes that we have a human need to transcend words and that music in worship can take us to a place that words never can. He thinks musical transcendence is something like directly hooking up the subconscious mind with the autonomic nervous system. He remembers attending a concert in which the slow movement from the Rachmaninoff Symphony No. 2 was played and thinking, "If only words could do that." For him, worship without music would be "irrational."

He urges caution when evaluating emotional response and transcendent experience in worship, however:

> I think we need to take a good look at the level and types of emotional response. I can be moved by *Old Yeller.* But I have to ask whether that is the same thing as religious experience. My fear is that we've found some pretty cheap ways of manufacturing an emotional response that we pass off as worshipful.

Then he relates his experience of going to another local church where the lights went down, the singers sang, the preacher preached, a video commercial was given for the next Sunday, they sang some more, and people left. As the lights came up and people were filing out, somebody said, "I feel like I've been to the movies." He finds this an interesting comment—a lot of movies move him emotionally, just as a lot of songs on the radio do. But what is the relationship between that emotion and what happens in worship? Sometimes he is puzzled at the profundity of a popular song in contrast to the lack of emotional profundity in "correct" worship. He believes we need to think and ask more questions about our worship.

The music director, for whom this church is a first long-term Presbyterian experience, responds on a more practical level. He says that the capacity for music to be vital in worship depends on the willingness of the senior pastor to work with the musician as a team member. He adds that no matter the view of music in worship, if teamwork is present, it is possible to discuss what worship leaders are trying to accomplish in the worship service and what music can best support that focus.

The music director discussed how the congregation views its role in music in Presbyterian worship. He said this congregation appreciates the singing of hymns that fit the Scriptures of the day, not just those hymns that worshipers know well, and that they want to sing the Psalter. He noted that he had an entirely new sense of the anthem's purpose after 9/11 when the congregation expressed how vital a part of the worship experience the choir's anthems were. That insight changed how he chooses the anthems and how he fits them into the worship service.

The organist speaks to the importance of addressing congregational participation:

> I think that some of the most important parts of the service are where the people physically, verbally participate. Hymn singing provides that opportunity. Music encourages people to enter into the worship experience more fully. Music provides people an opportunity to corporately express praise and thanksgiving, and sorrow as well as joy—the entire spectrum of our spiritual and emotional lives.

Here we see a gifted worship planning team whose members view music in Presbyterian worship from various perspectives, including that of the congregation, and who work together with a common purpose to design worship that calls for active involvement.

The Best Leader Is a Servant Leader

All the team members have a similar understanding of what it means to be a leader. The pastor believes a good Christian leadership model is that of a servant-leader, one that is collegial and emphasizes service rather than control. He likes to draw an organizational chart as an inverted pyramid. Given that, he believes his job to be providing resources for the people on the next tier, so they can do their job well. He thinks this is a more suitable model for church than the corporate model. He still retains the responsibility of his position, however: "This does not mean that I don't have authority, and I may need to say, 'This will not happen.' In doing that fairly, I am serving and taking responsibility as the primary custodian of the overall vision of the church." In this case, that servant-leader provides for the worship life of the church.

The pastor reflects specifically on music leadership, noting the vital balance between the human side of ministry requiring "people skills" and the musical skills required to produce great music for worship. He believes the most effective church musicians combine strong pastoral ministry with the abilities of good technical musicians:

> The best musicians in my congregation are the leaders who stretch their people beyond what they think they can do. They take people just to the edge of their capabilities and then stretch them to the point where they can do it, at which point the people say, "Wow!" It is an art to know how to do that. Frequently music leaders either take them not far enough, and you have a sort of pedantic approach, or they take them too far, and they're frustrated. An artist knows the balance.

He continues to reflect on the musician's many roles. First, there is the pedagogical aspect—teaching the singing, the liturgy, the text, including those texts of the music of our past that is great literature and important to our faith heritage. That is the rational side. Then the musician must also convey the best of the human spirit that is uniquely expressed in music. Music feeds the growth of the spirit and the development of the spiritual life. In the music director, he believes, you want a balance of those two things, the musical pedagogue and the spiritual caregiver. He has experienced situations when one or the other aspect was missing:

> One musician I worked with was probably the best organist I have ever heard—a true artist. But he found working with people so difficult that on Monday morning I would have to minister to his wounds after somebody looked at him the wrong way after the postlude on Sunday. On the other hand, I've known people who were very good with people but who had perfunctory music skills.

He thinks churches sometimes try to achieve a professional performance level at the expense of relationships, or may sacrifice a worthy musical product when the focus on the musical task is lost or the musician's skills are found wanting. It is the balance that is important.

The music director thinks the statement "Wait for me— I'm your leader" is not always a bad one. A good leader can empower people to do something significant. He thinks it is important for a leader to assist in others' growth both in their faith journeys and their musical abilities and to get out of the way and let them "do their thing," whatever it is. He sees his own role as enabling others:

> I have some skills as a singer and sing in a professional chamber group in town, but I don't sing in church. I think it's really important to give other people opportunity to sing who want to share their gifts. It would be easy for me to do a lot of solos, but I think that takes away from the ministry of others.

Musicians, he says, provide a quiet but significant kind of leadership when they intersect with members of the congregation at important life junctures. He says of the organist, "She works with families in grief in choosing music for memorial services. She plans celebrations of marriage. Part of being a professional church musician is helping people in major events in their lives." The music of these events is chosen as the organist draws from the family's musical memory and the repertoire of the congregation, shaping a new musical memory associated with those occasions that will become part of the family's traditions.

The music director reflects on being a member of a team at the church, which requires going to session (congregational governing body) meetings and participating in various committees in the church. It's a way to learn what else is going on and to be a part of the whole church. That teamwork carries over into the choir, where a structure is in place to care for choir members. "When we have someone in the hospital, we have a team that visits and takes flowers. It's very Presbyterian. It's very organized—who gets flowers, who gets cards. But the intention is to be there for people." At the end of our conversation, he was going to see someone in the hospital. "Some musicians would think that I'm crazy—and I guess I am. It says something about our priorities. The music is important, but it's not the most important thing. The people are the most important thing."

The organist describes a good leader as someone who encourages, who is sensitive to people's needs, and who is professionally prepared to respond to those needs. As a church musician, she believes a good leader, by meeting needs and giving encouragement, motivates people to participate in the life of the church, whether as a part of the choir or other musical group, or as a part of the singing congregation. The job of the church musician is to inspire people always to do their best. The good leader finds the "fine line" between always demanding perfection from the choir and settling for "second best." This is not easy when the musician is working with volunteers, who may range from professionals to those who can't read music. But she sees it as the role of the professional to encourage people to use whatever gifts they have, to find a way to help them contribute in whatever ways they can. Regarding the pastoral aspect of music-making in community, she finds the way the adult choir members care for one another remarkable. They share leadership as needs arise, focusing not on who is in charge but on whether a member is cared for.

Empowering the Congregation, Empowered by It

Presbyterians are described as governing themselves "decently and in order" for good reason, in that the governing bodies of the local and national church are usually highly structured and participatory. This church is no exception. But for the system to work well, the people must trust the system and one another.

Asked how the congregation enables him to lead, the pastor responds, "The big issue is trust, which is earned with time. My observation is that it takes five years in place for this to be optimal—a long five years!" If the congregation has created an environment that makes it possible for members to worship the way they do, he thinks that achievement is due to "a long history of faithful pastoral leadership, and a developed understanding and appreciation for Reformed worship."

The pastor believes the congregation has come to see music as a vital, integral component of worship that goes hand in hand with the proclaimed Word. Careful planning ensures that the music, the preaching, and the liturgy work together. The congregation believes in the ability of the music staff to make decisions about what constitutes high-quality music in worship. The long history of excellent music in worship at the church has given the congregation confidence to invest resources in maintaining this level of quality in music for worship; members know it is a *good* investment. The congregation also sees itself in the historic role of "patron of the arts," encouraging excellent music and conserving it for the community. Members are committed to quality partly because a trusted segment of the congregation is educated in music and can guide decision-making, and partly because music is an important part of most of the members' lives. Supporting music and musicians at the church is a long-standing priority and part of the congregational identity.

The organist, in particular, feels a great deal of responsibility for congregational song and spends much time preparing to lead the parts of the worship service that the congregation will sing. She thinks carefully about how to use the organ to illumine the meaning of a hymn text, using registration to interpret text with sound. For instance, references to the devil in "A Mighty Fortress Is Our God" might be made more real by using the strident reeds. In preparing hymns for worship, she thinks of how the congregation will sing them, considering singers' breathing, determining a tempo that is appropriate to convey the mood, style, and text of the hymn. Sometimes the plan will change in the course of a hymn, because she must listen to the congregation's singing and decide whether she needs to change registration, volume, or tempo to encourage the worshipers. She is clear about her role: "My goal is to encourage people to sing. I don't want to make it a contest between the congregation and the organ. This is a great singing congregation, and that's what's so rewarding. They encourage me, and I think I encourage them." While the congregation participates actively in the spoken responses of the liturgy, she thinks the high moments of communal worship are in the singing "when all of us are collectively 'carried away' by the power of singing praises to God." In this church the primary organ console used for worship is located between the choir and the congregation, so she can hear the enthusiastic singing of both contingents and considers herself "the leader of congregational song."

A democratic governance structure offers ways of addressing issues that may be difficult for leaders to address on their own. The music director recalls a time early in his tenure when one or two insistent people were saying, "We need to be doing more contemporary Christian music and doing a contemporary service." The leadership was not certain how to address this issue, but an opportunity presented itself. About that time the denomination sponsored a group that was touring the country to show churches how to do contemporary worship. The musicians came to town, and the music director thought, "Oh, this is going to be a disaster. People are going to want this." They came and led a service. When they left, everyone was politely saying, "That is *not* what we want."

From the perspective of the leaders, the visit was the best thing that could have happened, because it demonstrated the gap between what the congregation values and what this group offered. It helped the church to define itself. The music director believes in staying in this congregation's niche: "We're doing what we know how to do well, and we're growing steadily, bringing in a lot of families with young children, and it just seems to be a very healthy growth trend. So, I think that whatever we're doing seems to be working."

The congregation is supportive of the current leadership. Some members are concerned about what might happen when the current pastor or musicians retire. Will there be future musicians and pastoral candidates with similar formation and values to carry on leadership of the worship and the music program? Because the Presbyterian Church is congregationally determined and the Presbyterian seminaries are not consistent in their teaching of worship and music, these concerns carry some validity.

Vatican II Ideals

The musicians and pastor work hard to design worship in which music is an integral part of the liturgy. Their similar backgrounds, ease in communication, strategic planning processes, and appreciation for music all provide an environment where music and liturgy are inseparable. And all are working for the full, conscious, and active participation of the people. The music director notes the history of a previous music director who set the stage for this to happen. He especially encouraged congregational singing and the singing of the psalms, a legacy that is still felt years later. The music director observes, "This is a singing congregation. We don't just use the same old hymns all of the time. We always try newer hymns that may not be so familiar, but we want the congregation to sing. We want them to 'take home' that music."

Part of encouraging the people's participation has meant changing the wall surfaces and using paint that reflects sound to create as warm an acoustic atmosphere as possible for the size of the room. That has encouraged participation not only for the sung parts of the service but also for the spoken parts. The music director feels excitement when he hears people saying things like, "I never really wanted to sing before, but now I can't wait."

RESOURCES

Each team member regards the sanctuary itself as a major resource for the making of music, for both the congregation and the choirs. But coming to agreement on the space arrangement and acoustical needs required a long journey. The pastor remembers an era when it was frustrating to play an instrument in the sanctuary, because the carpet absorbed so much sound. But now instrumentalists say it is a joy to play there, because they can hear both themselves and one another. The church has found itself nurturing a "parish of musicians" from among the professionals in the community. Many of them express their love for this church, even though they are not members.

Getting to this point was neither quick nor easy. Acousticians have been consulted three times in the recent history of the church. Every time they said, "Take out all the carpeting." Twice the congregation said, "Thank you so much for your opinion," but kept the carpet. The third time the leadership decided to take up the carpet but only because the session was willing to make a decision that was pretty unpopular with a sizeable portion of the congregation. One person said to the pastor, half-kidding, half-serious, "If you take up that carpeting, I'll leave the church." But the session made the decision because its members realized that the overall acoustic environment would be improved. Another change was to move the choir down front. The founding pastor believed the choir should sit in the back of the sanctuary, because the choir represents the congregation in worship, rather than functioning as a performing group. The current pastor identifies two understandings at work in the placement of the choir. One says, "The choir is the opposite of a child: it should be heard but not seen." The other says that when we worship, we see one another gathered around the table. The decision was to change the location of the choir, so not only was it visible to the congregation, but also the communion table was between the choir and congregation, giving the sense of the entire community gathering around the table.

As a result of these changes, the choir has grown significantly, and the congregation has the experience of being a "singing body" rather than individuals who hear themselves sing. The rich environment for singing created another problem, however. The acoustics that enhanced singing rendered speech less clear. With more resonance in the room, understanding spoken words was more difficult. The congregation struggled to find technicians who could move the worship space from "acceptable" to "excellent" acoustics for speaking. People were concerned when someone said, "We can hear a lot better on the radio" (the 11:00 service is broadcast), "so we may as well stay home." New technology prevailed, and a new speaker system made possible a pleasant balance between acoustic needs for music and preaching.

As to the monetary and physical resources to sustain the program, the music budget is approximately 4 percent of the church budget, excluding all salaries. In addition to the program budget, staff members get $1,000 per year for continuing education and then contribute personal funds to make up the difference for travel to a national conference. Funds are available for the organist and ensemble leaders to buy music. Sometimes church members provide special gifts for the purchase of specific anthems or for other musical purposes, a practice that "supplements the budget tremendously."

Growth in the music program has been steady for a decade.

Year	*Participants in Music Program*
1998	150
2002	195 (new facilities dedicated in this year)
2008	296

Because the church is in an urban setting, professional musicians and groups, as well as faculty and students from a nearby university with a church music program, contribute significantly to the congregation's music program.

Building the Future

Several years ago, the church decided to hire a full-time staff member to address children's music and to lead the handbell choirs. The goals for the program include helping the children develop an understanding of worship in addition to presenting worthy, well-prepared music to the glory of God in worship. The program for children has grown into a graded choir program for ages four through kindergarten, first and second grades, and third through sixth grades. Each group rehearses for forty-five minutes every Sunday morning during the school year. Each choir has a curriculum for music skill development and worship/spiritual development. By the time the children are in sixth grade, they have not only learned to read music and acquired basic singing skills, but have also learned a basic repertoire of hymns and understand the seasons of the church year, the liturgical parts of the service, the biblical sources for the anthems they sing, the communal nature of church, the leadership role of choirs in worship, and the capacity of music to enable worshipers to respond to God. The children's and adult handbell choirs usually play music based on hymn tunes, which the director explores with the group to help the bell ringers understand the relationship between the text and the way the composer translates that text into sound.

TRADITION IN BALANCE

The congregation views the music program as an integral piece of the overall mission and history of the church. The music program today is as an outgrowth of the congregation's past and relates to the rest of the programming and outreach of the church.

The pastor spoke about the "Carol Sing," which began as an informal gathering in the youth house and became more formal when it moved into the sanctuary. There is a continuing effort to reinforce the congregation's ownership of the music and yet to provide an environment that enables the choir and other musicians to lead the congregation in its worship.

The music director tries to provide musical offerings that "people can count on." Several times a year, the choir sings evening programs, including a concert of American music in the summer. These special events provide an outreach to the community and an opportunity for church members to invite their friends to enjoy the music of the church regardless of their primary church commitments.

The church has significant commitments to service projects and sometimes asks musicians to help. When volunteers were needed to work on a health fair for one of the missions in town, cantors led "Jesu, Jesu, Fill Us with Your Love," a hymn with the theme of serving others, as part of an announcement in a worship service. When a retirement home asked for music to use with Alzheimer's patients, the choir recorded a compact disc with sixteen hymns. Others learned about the project and wanted copies to take to friends in hospice and hospital, and to a nursing home where the worship services lacked accompaniment for singing hymns. So a second recording session was scheduled with a larger and more representative selection of hymns, with the recording engineer volunteering his services.

Liturgical Pieties

The pastor believes that, in general, Presbyterians have a rather cerebral piety and are inspired by intellectual understanding. He understands this piety because he experiences it himself:

> If I hear a great lecture, and someone describes something I never could have verbalized that way, I end up saying, "Yeah!" On some level I may have sensed it, but hearing it explained just turns all my bells on. It is powerful. So if a sermon can enlighten the situation of someone's life and the life of the world with a biblical text, that's a favorite of Presbyterians.

He contrasts cerebral piety with the piety of mystery, a sensing that there is more going on in this moment than can be explained. He describes these approaches in terms of personality types: the "Intuitives" in the world love mystery, and the "Sensors" want things explained to them. He has to be careful how he preaches. Because of his intuitive leaning, he is inclined just to paint the picture. But the frustrated "Sensors" will ask, "What are you trying to tell us here?" So he tries to balance the sensing side, or the conscious, cerebral piety that is seeking understanding, with the kind of intuitive piety that says, "Tell me there is more meaning to my life than I often feel there is."

He then explains how music can reflect both pieties: "Choral music or hymns that are based on a biblical text and that tell a story speak to the cerebral piety. Music that does not have text or has text that is suggestive rather than concrete speaks more to the mystery and imagination. Both pieties are important." He further explains that the church has tried to use different kinds of musical resources to build meaningful worship that includes both pieties.

The music director affirms the importance of the cerebral piety, knowing the congregation is astute and well educated. He thinks the text is *always* important, but he has also chosen less text-driven anthems and other music that were received positively as well.

The organist explains how she works with music that has no text and chooses it for the meaning it may evoke. She asks questions such as: For prelude music, will this encourage the congregation to begin worship? Will this music help create a space for the Holy Spirit to enter? Does the music reflect the liturgical sense of season, and where possible, the specific focus of the sermon and biblical texts? For postlude music, does the music encourage the congregation to leave with joyful thanksgiving and a sense of purpose for the week ahead?

Accentuating the Positive

The organist remarks that the staff has never experienced conflicts in which pastors requested music that musicians felt they could not offer with integrity. Rather, she believes the musicians are a valued part of the staff and respected for their contributions to the decision-making for worship.

The music director jokes with the organist that her middle name is "Flexible," so when something doesn't work the way they think it's going to, they just make the best of it. A team of volunteers helps enormously to fill in gaps when otherwise things might go very wrong. For example, three volunteers work every week in the music library. The music director says, "We'd be *sunk* if we didn't have the volunteers to do that work, and they are people who love doing it."

He goes on to talk about the environment:

Really, it's a great place to be—fewer complainers, fewer grip-ers—and I've had some good ones! I can think of a couple of specific instances at a church where people would come into the church and try to go through a list of all the things I needed to do differently. And that wears you down and takes a lot of patience. It's so great not to have that kind of thing going on here. Every once in a while, someone might make a suggestion or something, but that's fine.

The positive atmosphere gives volunteers and participants in the music program a sense of ownership in the program, and they are quick to help prevent something from going wrong or to remedy something when it does go wrong. Their spirits are indomitable.

Minds, Hearts, and Voices in Sync

Presbyterians have a reputation for valuing the life of the mind in worship and for running their affairs "decently and in order." Those qualities are evident in this church. What this congrega-tion has done through the music program, however, is to balance these hallmarks of mainline Presbyterianism with "heart." The investment in a sanctuary with good acoustics for both speak-ing and singing, a superb organ, a music library and rehearsal facilities, musicians with skill and pastoral sensitivity, a chil-dren's program to build for the future, together with a pastor who works collegially for integrated liturgy—the combination of these has resulted in holistic worship. The congregation responds with engaged minds, spirits, and enthusiastic partici-pation in the music of worship. Further, the worship empowers the life of the church into social action in the world beyond. This is worship that engages mind, heart, voice—all of one's be-ing—in praise and prayer. It is real. It is good. It lasts.

All Good Things

CHAPTER 9

In the End,
What Really Matters

THIS CONGREGATION OF THE PRESBYTERIAN CHURCH (USA) has eighty to ninety members and about forty in attendance on any Sunday morning. The church was formerly known for both a rich worship tradition and active community participation. But members have gradually given up most of their outreach activities as they have grown older. Now they focus on their vital worship and communal life together. The changing neighborhood and schools in this part of the city once motivated the congregation to offer extensive programming for neighborhood children, as well as English as a second language (ESL) classes. The church still offers classrooms for others to teach ESL classes and shares its space with a congregation that worships in Spanish later on Sunday morning. It funds building operations for both independent congregations from earnings on an endowment and the continuing generosity of the members. The English-language congregation, the subject of this study, has an older contingent that has been welcoming to gays and lesbians, some of whom are their children. The church retains a pastor, an organist who also functions as the office manager, and a part-time choir director. The choir of ten to fifteen members rehearses weekly and provides music for worship every week. Despite declining membership, the church has decided to put most of its resources into retaining strong leadership, placing great emphasis on high-quality music and liturgy in worship. As members say, "We've never been able to define how to do church halfway—we cannot stop being who we are." Their music and worship define them. The congregation sings frequently and enthusiastically in worship.

Organized in 1890, the church has a history of strong music, including the influence of a major church-music composer whose family has been associated with the life of the congregation. People say they sing in the choir because of the high quality of music they are able to produce. The congregation knows music and is quick to notice if the music is not up to its usual standard. The liturgy is thoughtfully prepared and alternates between carefully chosen spoken words (liturgical and homiletic) and hymnody, responses often chosen from hymns, and choral singing. Instrumental music is provided by a competent organist who is himself a composer, as well as by members who play instruments and guests who often come to contribute their musical gifts.

The current sanctuary, built in 1950, is a traditional rectangular structure with high ceilings and hard surfaces, providing an acoustically superb space for singing. A pipe organ was installed, using most of an organ relocated from a college campus and refitted to serve the sanctuary. An excellent Yamaha grand piano is available in the sanctuary as well. Separate rooms for choir rehearsal/warm-up and a choral library provide ample space for the music program. A set of handbells is owned by the church but rarely used now.

On the Sundays of the site visits, I was astounded by the vitality of the singing. The sound fills the space completely, with many of the members singing the hymns in parts. Though members of the congregation have grown older and fewer, the music is clearly important to their worship. On one Sunday a member who is a pianist played for the offertory, and a different member played clarinet on another Sunday. The choir sang anthems both Sundays, while the creative and competent organist led hymns and responses, and provided transitions between parts of the liturgy. The congregation expressed warm affirmation for the musicians after both services.

The Leaders

The success of pastor and musicians in helping this congregation retain its quality of music and worship rests in their strong personal and professional respect for each other, their mutual commitments to high-quality music, their creative yet practical planning for worship, and the involvement of so many members in the music-making.

JOB DESCRIPTIONS

The pastor preaches and is in charge of all the worship planning in coordination with the worship and congregational life committee. She will frequently fill in as soprano or alto, depending on what is needed, for choir anthems or special music. Besides playing the organ and organizing the music for services, the organist serves as office manager for the church. He is adept at recruiting talent from both within and outside the church to participate in the music of worship. The choir director plans the choral music, leads rehearsals, and teaches English as a second language.

MUSICAL FORMATION OF PASTOR AND MUSICIANS

The pastor experienced early years filled with music, with her mother playing the piano, singing in the choir, and providing recorded music of all kinds in the home. The pastor studied piano and voice and sang in church choirs through high school. She began college as a music major, and though she switched majors after three years, still continued to study music through graduate school. A seminal experience for her during high school was to serve on the worship and music committee at her church, where she experienced the planning that structured the worship life of the church. As to the place of music in her life, she says, "Music has always been meaningful to my life . . . intellectually and also part of my spiritual journey."

The musicians were more informally trained. The organist grew up playing by ear as well as learning to sight-read; he composes prolifically. He says his interest in music was discovered when he began playing tunes on the piano by ear at age four. His mother sacrificed to make sure he had piano lessons, so that he gained skills in reading music to match his natural ability to hear music.

The choir director has a master's degree in religious education and studied voice extensively. His father was a Baptist preacher, so he grew up experiencing the music of the church. He started as a music major in college but dropped it when he could not seem to make progress with his voice teacher. It was only later in seminary that he encountered a voice teacher who helped him recognize that as a singer, he was a tenor and not a baritone, despite his lower speaking voice. This knowledge opened new musical horizons for him.

The backgrounds of the pastor and the musicians give them a common language with which to communicate easily, and a common love for good music that spills over into their work together in planning and implementing music for worship.

Working and Planning Together

The pastor and the musicians have open, easy relationships and feel free to offer ideas and comments to each other. According to PCUSA polity, responsibility for worship rests with the pastor, but she readily receives all suggestions from the musicians, objecting only when she believes that the ideas don't fit with the overall liturgical plan for the day or when the music may be too complex for the congregation's musical resources. Since the pastor has as much musical training as the musicians, or more, they work together almost as equals in the planning and implementation. But the pastor is quick to change a course of action in the planning session if she feels it does not serve the overall goals of the service. The musicians respect her right to make changes and also respect her musicianship. At work are a strong administrative pastor and creative, artistic musicians.

Planning sessions of pastor and musicians are held approximately every three months. I was able to attend one of these planning sessions and observed the friendly working relationships. The pastor provided the outline for the lectionary and liturgical calendar, as well as planning guides. The musicians worked creatively to suggest congregational and choral music. They welcomed me into the discussions and the singing in four-part harmony of choral octavo options for several months of Sundays. While much was accomplished, it was obvious that this meeting was a labor of love by colleagues who enjoyed one another and were committed to the task at hand. The meeting was in the choral office, so hymnals, liturgical music, and choral files were close at hand.

Evaluation of liturgies occurs more informally, when the office manager/organist, pastor, and choir director are in the church at the same time. Feedback from the congregation also happens informally, generally after the service on a Sunday morning.

The pastor has final responsibility for putting the worship service together, as stated in the *Book of Order*. She works with the worship and congregational life committee, which provides general direction for worship in each liturgical season and secures ushers and liturgists. The pastor provides their training. She says about the music, "As far as the music [is concerned], my official responsibility is just to pick the hymns. I know that in a lot of congregations the pastor leaves that to the music director, but since I have a music background, I like to do that." She identifies the theological concepts for the liturgy and the sermon from the Scriptures, and chooses hymns that coordinate with those theological themes.

Views of Music in Liturgy

The pastor has thought deeply about the relationship between theology and music, and she believes music can bring a dynamic to worship that is missing with only the spoken word. She comments: "I think the place of music in the liturgy is to give people a means to offer their praise and worship, and an additional way in which to 'catch theology.' Most of us 'catch theology' better through hymns than we do from just listening to sermons. It is the theology contained in the music that we often remember." Further, she takes seriously the importance of choosing high-quality hymnody, because a text associated with music is more easily remembered. She asks questions such as: Is the text theologically appropriate? Is the melody singable? Is the melody expressive of the text?

The pastor has also thought about the concepts of music as performance and music as an offering in liturgy. She finds persuasive philosopher/theologian Søren Kierkegaard's idea that it is not the preacher and the choir who are performers, and the congregation that is the audience. Rather, all of us are the performers, and God is the audience. The music is a part of that performance, part of the work of the people. Further, she explains how the choir anthem can be understood in this model. Sometimes a choir is seen as a performing entity with the congregation as the audience. But this congregation understands that the choir is offering music on its behalf; the congregants offer their listening, and all is offered to God.

The choir director and organist talk about the power of music to serve as a vehicle for the worship of this congregation in particular. Because music is so important to the members, music is the effective carrier of the content of any worship service. While they acknowledge the importance of the liturgy and spoken word, they also know that it is the music that will speak most eloquently to the members of this congregation.

The pastor and both musicians understand that their individual roles have the most significance, however, when they fit together into the whole. Rather than focusing on the merit of individual pieces, the pastor suggests the evaluation should be: "Did the music and the prayers and the sermon all fit together in a way that let people worship? That's what matters."

WHAT MAKES FOR A GOOD LEADER?

The pastor and musicians talk about the importance of both musical and theological knowledge, and the ability to work with the people in leading worship that fully engages the congregation. The knowledge of the congregation itself is key, according to the pastor: "I think a good leader is someone who has learned how to read people well enough to know when to pull them, when to push them, and when you just have to get out of the way." This ability, she says, requires enough self-knowledge, ego strength, and selflessness to affirm others who do things well, and the willingness to let them have the credit for it. She quotes her father: "One of the wisest things I heard my dad say is that it is amazing how much you can accomplish if you don't care who gets credit."

Music leadership builds on these same principles, the pastor observes. A music leader has to have the musical knowledge to be discerning about the quality of a tune—even if discernment of quality was part of the process of selecting hymns for publication in a hymnal, not all tunes may be appropriate for a given congregation. The musical ability and the perspectives of the congregation need to be taken into account. What are these worshipers' capabilities? How are they likely to respond to the music? Beyond that, a music leader needs to know whether a text is "good theology."

Another aspect of good music leadership is to provide inspiration for the musical portion of the liturgy. The organist quotes a church-musician colleague who also conducts the local symphony chorus: "The church music department, in the best-case scenario, should act as the cheerleaders for the congregation. We are the ones who lead them in the praise of God." If music involves all of our being—mind, body, spirit, emotion—then the leader of music must view the task of leadership as one of engaging the totality of what it means to be human.

ON WORKING TOGETHER

The pastor and the musicians have an easy relationship with one another, respect one another's abilities, and are able to focus on the task at hand quickly and effectively. The musical training of the pastor and the theological training of the musicians give them a common language and understanding of both realms that make their work together unique. The pastor observes her situation in contrast to that of her colleagues: "I guess one of the differences is that I don't see the musicians as being my adversaries. I have known pastors who did feel that way. And I've known musicians who, through experience, have felt that pastors were their adversaries and that you always had to fight over turf." She believes her training in music allows her ease in working with musicians.

This ease in relationship does not mean that the pastor shirks her responsibility for the full worship service. The overall responsibility for worship and for the administration of the church still is in her domain. She explains:

> I'm responsible for looking ahead on the calendar and seeing what's coming up, making sure that the planning takes place, making sure that we stay within the budget for buying music, or tuning, or getting soloists. And every now and then, I have to tell them, "No, you can't do that, because we're out of money." I rarely ever tell them a definitive no, however. I might say, "Can we please do that on a different Sunday instead?" I tend to be the one with the larger picture in mind, aware of where things fit and where they should go. But, in general, we take suggestions from each other, in terms of music and liturgy.

The choir director acknowledges that he and the organist tend to be the creative partners in the team. He says the pastor "is very good at being well organized. It's not always clean and pretty, but we do balance each other." He says further, "We do not have the arguments that other churches do. To me, it is a conversation."

Thinking of their own positive experiences and the difficulties in other situations, the pastor reflects on how pastors and musicians ideally could be trained:

> From my own experience, there is no substitute for pastors having at least some musical training and church musicians having some theological training. We can't send every church musician to seminary to get a master's degree in sacred music, nor is every pastor going to be able to take piano lessons or voice lessons. Some have a real appreciation for music, and some don't. Seminaries are being asked to do more and more these days, and I recognize that. But it would be so helpful for pastors to see the liturgy through the eyes of the musician and for musicians to see what they are doing in the church from a theological view and not simply as musical performance, technique, and theory.

The ability to share a common language has given the staff the opportunity to share books pertinent to their work and to discuss them. Or the musicians may offer a recording or a piece of music for the pastor to take home to see whether it could work for worship. The ability to communicate is at the core of how they work, according to the pastor: "To use each other's language seems to me to be awfully important. The congregation notices it—not always consciously. But they notice whether things fit together or they don't. You can't make worship fit together if you haven't learned to speak a little of each other's language." The common language is what enables the relationships to work, and

the relationships allow the gifts of all to be used most effectively
to produce a coherent, integrated worship.

A Congregation that Lives and
Breathes through Music

As the members of the congregation have aged, many have
moved to a retirement community in the area. They continue
their active involvement in the church as long as they can. The
organist at the church comes to the retirement community to
entertain after dinner at least once a month. He is also involved
in the local theater-organ society, and once members organized
an outing to an outlying town to hear him play his own composition for a silent movie being shown in a town hall. Monthly
dinners for the congregation often include some form of musical entertainment, whether by the staff or others. Hymn singing
may accompany an ice cream social, or a music program might
not have a sacred component at all. For this congregation, music is a way of bringing members together, even for those who
don't sing or dance or play an instrument, but especially for
those who do. It is a way they give to the others, a way of sharing
themselves, a way of making an offering of who they are. But the
primary focus of the music in the life of the congregation is its
worship every Sunday morning.

The church members are concerned about the congregation's
future. The church is in a part of the city that is not considered safe anymore; the members are at an age when outreach
programs to respond to the neighborhood would require an
energy they no longer have; and the economic needs and lack
of leadership in the immediate neighborhood raise questions as
to whether a local congregation could sustain a ministry. At this
point, the members can sustain the operations of the church
from an endowment and the ability of the membership to give
generously. The pastor puts their priorities into perspective: "I
think that this congregation, even if they reach a point where
they don't have professional music staff, will still be a singing

congregation." She observes that many congregations would already have given up a choir and might have gone to using volunteers for music leadership. But for now, of all the choices the members have to make, they are placing their worship life at the top of the list.

About Vatican II Ideals

Again, because of her dual background in music and theology, the pastor was able to reflect on a discussion of the Vatican II instructions for music in worship. She believes these goals have been a part of Protestant worship since the time of the Reformation, because Calvin and Luther both insisted that music was an integral part of the liturgy and that music should be sung by all. That is, they would certainly have endorsed Vatican II's call for the "full, active, and conscious participation" of the laity in worship. But she also believes Protestants have learned through this time of focus on liturgical change about the importance of uniting word and sacrament. She also affirms the importance of lay participation in worship:

> If the congregation isn't participating in the liturgy, then it isn't really *liturgy—leitourgia*—the work of the people. It may be a performance by the priest or pastor. It may be private devotions by everyone present. But it isn't *liturgy*. Music is one means by which congregants participate in the liturgy.

She appreciates the reminder in the Vatican II documents that music is necessary to the liturgy and that it should be integrated into the liturgy, not an adjunct to it. "I have difficulty with the 'fifteen minutes of praise' that some contemporary services begin with. . . . It seems to me to be the equivalent of sending out a warm-up act before the *real* performer gets on stage. Too often, it doesn't seem to have anything to do with what follows." Indeed, she believes, the Vatican II documents are helpful to Protestants in understanding the *purpose* of music in liturgy.

The Music Program

The budget lines for music are adequate for the current program, with $500 for choral music to augment an already fine choral library, $1,500 for organ/piano maintenance, and $1,250 for guest musicians' honoraria. Any long-term organ maintenance is capitalized over a period of years to be paid from designated building funds. The pastor has an extensive library of hymnals from a variety of denominations, and the staff uses a mix of planning resources, including *Prepare* from the United Methodist Church and *Call to Worship* from the Presbyterian Church (USA). Local seminary and music libraries are rich resources. The public library has a good music collection, and a music store with adequate inventory is available. Because the region has many fine church music programs, the staff and libraries of other churches offer another source of music resources. There are also active chapters of the American Choral Directors Association and the American Guild of Organists in the area. There has been a sense in this congregation that worship that is done right is done well, and leaders always find the resources to make sure that it is done well.

A Tradition of Cherishing Their Music

The congregation has long cherished and nurtured its music. When asked why this has been so, a member responded, "Our church was fortunate in having pastors, assistant pastors, choir directors, and organists who were musicians or who loved music." Indeed, the church leadership and families within the church included significant professional and talented lay musicians who not only contributed musical skills, but also helped to build a music library of substance and acquired instruments with a view to their long-term use.

The story of how the pipe organ came to reside at this church is an example of the commitment to quality in the congregation's music offerings. A member's son knew of an organ that was being dismantled at a college in an adjacent state to make room for a new installation. Church members decided this was an opportunity not to be missed, and in the early 1970s, they rented four trucks to bring the organ to the church. A relative of one of the members was hired to do the installation, along with much help from members and a fund drive among the membership that helped with the costs. Miniature replicas of the organ made by woodworkers in the congregation were given to those who helped with the funding and serve as reminders of the story. Water damage in 1995 necessitated extensive rebuilding of the organ. Again, miniature organ models were crafted by a member out of wood salvaged from the damaged wind chests, and the replicas were used to recognize those who helped with repairs. The yearly budget of the church has always included a maintenance fund for the organ with an ongoing fund balance for maintenance that is required only periodically.

The cherishing of the congregation's tradition includes openness to new ways of worshiping and making music. One member recalls the introduction of the new *Presbyterian Hymnal* in the 1990s. While many churches were reluctant to make the change, this congregation welcomed the new hymnal. Asked why this was so, the member said the new hymnal offered opportunities to learn new music and to make the music of congregational worship better.

The pastor describes rituals that the congregation has come to expect, such as singing the psalm every Sunday, as well as singing everything possible in the liturgy as a congregation rather than having the pastor speak or the choir sing on behalf of the congregation. That practice was borne out in my observation of the worship services. Though a published musical setting of service music by a single composer may not be used, the liturgy is sung by using short settings of the liturgical parts or stanzas of hymns, creating a coherent, sung liturgy.

The staff and congregation are thinking a lot these days about traditions and how they have changed over the years, as they also reflect on what their future might be. For example, a traditional hanging-of-the-greens service has gone by the wayside as fewer people were interested in the activity and children were not present to encourage such a service. A Service of Lessons and Carols on Christmas Eve is still a tradition, beginning with "Once in Royal David's City" and including "Silent Night," first in German and then in English, with candles lit. Singing Handel's "Hallelujah" chorus at the close of the Easter service is no longer possible because "we don't have the forces anymore."

Another tradition is to sing frequently the music of a major church music composer whose family has long been associated with the church. The library has copies of nearly all her works, which they sing when the appropriate liturgical day or lectionary Scripture coincides with the text of the work.

WHEN SOMETHING STOOD IN THE WAY

Churches are made up of fallible human beings, and things go wrong. Mistakes are made, difficult situations appear, and awkward moments in worship inevitably occur. How do leaders respond when something gets in the way of the positive work they would rather be doing? The organist describes a time when he felt he had to play for a singer. Everything in him did not want to do so, but he agreed anyway.

> And I was as cold and scientific about it as I could be. Until we got into the first refrain of the piece, and the Holy Spirit got hold of me and said, "What do you think you are doing? Who are you doing this for?" And I thought, "O, God, forgive me." And I turned on the other spigot and started being the best that I could be. It changed my life, because I was no longer allowing my ego to stand in the way.

The choir director describes a time when the organist was suddenly taken to the hospital, and he had to play for the service, even though he does not play well. The congregation sang really well that Sunday—perhaps, he thought, because the members wanted to make sure the music offering was the best it could be.

Both of these examples show leaders who believe that their work is greater than themselves and who are committed to the greater good, and a congregation whose members are committed to helping one another offer gifts of music that are the very best they can offer. Circumstances do not prevent them from giving their best. Only their best is good enough.

In the End, What Really Matters

This church is an example of how important music can be in unifying and focusing the life and worship of a group of people over their lifetimes. Even as this congregation is aging and the future of the church is in question, the integrity of the music and liturgy in worship supersedes all other considerations. Music may accompany their social functions and serve as entertainment in those settings. But when it is time for worship, there is no question about the role of music and how important it is to their praise and prayer.

Music and liturgy are woven seamlessly together from the beginning to the end of any worship service by a pastor and music staff who share musical and theological language. The congregants may not always understand the impact this cohesiveness has on their worship and may even respond primarily to the music—which is just fine. But it is the wedding of spoken and sung word that is spiritually powerful.

The congregation is actively involved in the music-making, from providing resources to engaging in committee work to offering musical skills to joining in enthusiastic congregational singing. The music is varied but always held to a high standard of quality by both the staff and the congregation. Despite uncertainty about the future of the church itself, this is a congregation with vibrant, joyful worship.

In the Garden

CHAPTER 10

Commonalities across Denominations and Contexts

ALL SITES IN THIS STUDY WERE CHOSEN BECAUSE OF THEIR demonstrated ability to fulfill two primary criteria articulated by the Second Vatican Council: (1) music and liturgy promote the "full, conscious, and active participation" of the people, and (2) music forms "a necessary and integral part of the solemn liturgy." Preceding chapters describe how these churches fulfilled the criteria and what factors have contributed to the reputations they enjoyed for having "good" music programs. Each congregation has defined "excellence" in its own context and serves as a model for others searching for ideas that have worked in venues similar to their own. Characteristics common to all the sites are the subject of this chapter.

Leaders Who Serve, Servants Who Lead

Catholic theologian Avery Dulles, in his 1974 book *Models of the Church,* includes a chapter titled "The Church as Servant." Dulles cites a document[1] prepared by Pope Paul VI that highlights what the author considers to be one of the most important contributions of Vatican II: a deeper understanding of the relationship of the church to the world. As Christ came to the world not to be served but to serve, the church is here to serve. In our study of nine churches that fulfilled the selected criteria from Vatican II, we found leaders who wanted to serve. They are examples of people who, though they may have authority by virtue of their positions, "do not rule by power but attract by love."[2]

When we began this study, the focus was intentionally *not* on leaders but rather on the churches that had sustained significant music programs over the years, led by numerous pastors and musicians. By choosing the sites in this way, we could ensure that it was the *congregations* that had sustained the music of their worship. We were interested in knowing about music programs that lasted.

As a practical matter, because our funding was limited and our research team was small, we talked to leaders at the sites. We attempted to capture a current snapshot of each church to identify how programs had developed in the past, and to determine how leaders are preparing for the future. Current leaders gave access to that information. When they were asked how they thought about leadership, models of servant leadership were mentioned again and again. Here are some of the ways the respondents described good leadership:

- The statement "Wait for me—I'm your leader" is not always a bad one. A good leader can empower people to do something really significant.
- Good Christian leadership is collegial and emphasizes service rather than control.
- A good leader is one who has an astute awareness of the community—one who delegates and builds community relationships and calls forth the gifts of the community.
- A good leader empowers others.
- An effective leader facilitates the good qualities in other people—draws out their strong qualities and lets them "fly with it."
- A good leader has an exceptional ability to listen.
- A good leader energizes those he or she is attempting to lead, leads by direction and by example, and is open to critique and respectful of the opinions of others.

- A good leader has learned to read people well enough to know when to pull them, when to push them, and when to just get out of the way.

- A leader has to be able to listen and take the pulse of those he or she is asked to lead. "You have to be courageous at times, and sometimes make hard calls. You have to listen, and you have to learn. You have to be willing to go back and admit when you are wrong. You have to appreciate people's gifts, and let them know that you appreciate them."

In every instance, the servant leadership characteristics of the clergy and musicians could be linked to their close connections with church experiences as children. They identified primary or extended family members, often in church leadership positions, and clergy or church musicians who modeled the importance of church and faith commitments. The mother or father who was an elder, the uncle who was a priest, the mother who gave the first piano lessons, the father who was a pastor, the church organist who led choir practice—these people were the first influences on these leaders. It was the *relationships* with people they respected that shaped their thinking about what was important. These relationships were not experienced as manipulative or controlling, but rather as loving, generous, selfless; these models went out of their way to nurture the interests and gifts of a young person in church.

The leaders interviewed also pointed to the influence of well-placed professionals along the way who recognized their gifts and often became mentors. These professionals provided opportunity for the future leader to train as an acolyte, to take piano lessons, to serve on a worship committee, to preach at church camp, to discern a call. These mentors even had the grace to acknowledge their own limitations and to send the young person for training beyond what they themselves could provide. The leaders we interviewed discerned their vocations with the people who meant much to them. Thus, clergy and musicians of the churches in this study were profoundly influenced by people who demonstrated servant leadership, who not only served as inspiring models to these young persons, but also selflessly identified gifts in others for leadership.

Music and Faith Formation of Leaders

As children, all these leaders experienced musical and faith formation in a church, even if it was of a faith tradition different from the one in which they now find themselves. Seven of the nine clergy and two of ten musicians were formed in the faith traditions where they now serve. Music and church were inseparable for all these leaders in their formative years.

Three of the ten musicians have degrees in which theology was part of the curriculum. Seven others have taken classes, attended workshops, or done reading in theology. Especially for non-Catholic musicians, musical competence rather than theological training is a primary requirement for employment. Musicians tended to move between denominations with relative ease, their tasks defined primarily as musical rather than pastoral or theological.

Four of the nine clergy interviewed had significant formal music education (private voice/piano lessons, college study in music), and eight of the nine had sung in children's choirs in church. All of them are able to read music. Two of ten musicians hold graduate degrees in church music. Six musicians completed graduate degree programs in organ or choral conducting from secular universities, and three have doctoral degrees. One has studied music outside a formal degree program. Although all leaders had early childhood experiences in church that influenced vocational paths, all also experienced music in other places, and some of the clergy have extensive music training. The common factor for both clergy and musicians is their early musical formation in the church itself.

Music of the church continues to be important to these leaders. For the musicians, in particular, their personal faith development and professional roles as church musicians are vitally linked. As one of the musicians said, "The mystery and drama of the liturgy gradually led to a 'spiritual awakening' that brought my understanding of theology and music into alignment." The clergy participate actively in music both in their congregations and in their communities.

Despite their busy lives, the musicians often contribute musically in professional circles outside the church (sing with professional choral groups, conduct professional choirs, perform organ recitals), and, in doing so, serve the greater community. They garner respect for both themselves and the church. They see themselves not only as *church* musicians but also as *professional* musicians and are held in esteem by their congregations for their dual reputations. Musicians who work in this way have opportunity to think carefully about the difference between working with professionals outside the church and with volunteers inside the church, about professional standards of music-making in secular settings, and about giving God the best in liturgical contexts.

No matter their denominational backgrounds, the musicians have redefined their standards of quality and excellence through education and work experiences. Three Episcopal, five Presbyterian, and one Catholic musician have moved from denominations with more informal liturgical and music traditions to denominations in which they now serve to offer music more closely aligned with their understanding of what it means to give God the best. Using high-quality music for worship is a matter of integrity for these musicians, and they are willing to expend great effort to teach this music to those who do not know it.

Clergy formed in their current denominations (three Catholic, one Episcopal, three Presbyterian) appreciate the best music in their traditions and believe this music to be the most appropriate vehicle for expressing prayer and praise. Two clergy who came from other traditions and are now Episcopalians appreciate the music of their present traditions. Though having adopted the more formal liturgy of the Episcopal tradition, they, unlike the musicians, often view music of the Episcopal tradition as interchangeable with music from their childhood faith traditions. While they would not adopt the more informal liturgical structures from the traditions that formed them, they will replace more formal music with that from other denominations or even nondenominational sources if they believe the congregation will relate to it more easily. Where music is concerned, pragmatic concerns may outweigh theological bases for decision-making.

Tenure of Musicians

A surprising discovery of the study is that eight of the ten musicians had been in the churches longer than the priests or pastors, and several of them had been in place for multiple changes of clergy. These musicians know the congregations well, and the congregations know them, having shared worship for years and planned music together for life passages—baptisms, weddings, funerals. The musician functions as extended family for members of congregations in some cases. The musicians in the study often see themselves as educators, either as conductors of groups or as teachers of adult education classes. They write articles for newsletters and provide background information on music for the worship bulletin. The musicians have a theologically and musically formative role in the lives of their congregations. They exercise significant influence, despite the fact that half of the musicians are part-time. Though most hold advanced degrees, they usually serve without benefits (such as health-insurance coverage or pension contributions) and without employment security in the church or the denomination.

How Musicians and Clergy Work Together

Musicians and clergy in this study work together by different methods, influenced by their backgrounds, current circumstances, and approaches to their tasks. But they find a means of working together.

The easiest and most efficient working arrangements are those where the clergy and musician share common theological and musical language and meet regularly to plan. Cross-training in theology and music is clearly advantageous. In the absence of dual training, working together with common understandings of the components of worship (using the same lectionary readings and liturgical outlines, for example) can achieve integration of music and liturgy.

The most common way of working together is through "dialogue." Dialogue, a genuine conversation, results in good communication between clergy and musician even when neither has substantial training in the other's field, provided they share an appreciation and respect for each other. This exchange of ideas allows them to use each other's gifts effectively. Most of our respondents work in consultation with each other and achieve remarkable results. Those interviewed report how much they learn from the other person when working in dialogue and how much they appreciate working together. Over time, their vocabulary and knowledge of the other field grows. To draw a comparison with professionals in another field, scientific researchers who bring individually unique expertise to the same research project might function similarly to the way these clergy and musicians approach their work together. Though the denomination's polity may establish the clergy member as the head of the team, as a practical matter these clergy/musician teams work as partners. Each brings different but equally important expertise to a common task.

Dealing with Conflict

Most of the leaders in the sites we visited experience conflict with each other at some point but resolve the conflict successfully. It is hard to pinpoint specific disagreements identified in interviews, because any significant conflict had been resolved long before. Details were forgotten or remembered differently. What is important is that the leaders focus on their common work together. A few general observations can be gleaned from the study, nevertheless.

The clergy and musicians who experience the smoothest and most productive working relationships embrace servant leadership styles in which their common tasks and respect for each other are the dominant factors. A collegial working style is enormously helpful—and, if this study is an indication, it is normative—in effectively combining two disciplinary fields (music and theology) that are needed to make coherent worship. Communication is easier when clergy and musicians share a common language and can talk more easily about common goals. Similar musical and theological formation as children and teenagers helps, too. But these similarities are not essential for good working relationships to exist. Rather, the willingness to respect and value the other's point of view and to learn from that person is the most important character trait. In fact, several teams mentioned how much they enjoyed learning from each other.

Some clergy voluntarily mentioned musician/clergy conflicts. The common factors in these cases are:

- The long tenure of the musician who had been in place prior to the arrival of the current priest or pastor.
- The more authoritarian leadership style of the clergy.
- The worship formation of the clergy in another faith tradition.
- A perceived lack of education in music for clergy and/or lack of clarity of roles for clergy and musician.

Clergy who see conflict as an issue said their vocations were initiated by a personal "call" rather than as a result of encouragement by a mentor or other individual in close relationship to them over a long period of time. These clergy tended toward more authoritarian leadership styles and were more likely to claim the authority of their position in making decisions, "pulling rank" when disagreements arose.

Where conflict was present and could not be resolved, clergy adapted to the musician only when they sensed a mandate from the congregation. Sometimes the clergy used the authority of the position to initiate alternative means of accomplishing goals, such as starting an alternative service with different musicians. At one site the process of the study brought to the surface latent issues so troublesome that the pastor with an authoritarian style of leadership chose to stop conversations and remove the site from the study late in the process.

Despite disagreements from time to time, the clergy person and musician in each of these nine sites have established ways of relating to each other that allow fulfillment of their professional roles. Some have a respectful working relationship that does not extend beyond the church. That is, they are colleagues but not best friends. Some are best friends who regularly do things together. Others rarely see each other because of busy schedules. The nature of the individual working arrangements does not seem to matter. All agree that their work together is important, and the personal relationship does not get in the way of the important task of providing meaningful worship for the people of God.

Congregational Input into Decision-Making

The involvement of the congregation is important in maintaining the music program in these sites. The nature of official church governance ranges from hierarchical (Catholic) to democratic (Presbyterian), with Episcopal governance in between. The "official" denominational structure and how governance works in the congregation can be very different, but perhaps surprisingly, one of the most active liturgy committees is in one of the Catholic churches. The bottom line is that the congregations are the driving force in these sites.

One important characteristic of church musicians, mentioned frequently by church members, is that their musician communicates well with lay musicians and the congregation. This quality includes understanding the musical aptitude of the congregation—how congregants sing, what hymns they know—and helping them understand how music functions in worship. The better the rapport the musician has with lay musicians and the congregation, the more informed congregants are when making decisions about the music program. Likewise, the musician is more able to make decisions on their behalf.

In maintaining good communication with their congregations, these musicians stand in contrast to a "performer" model of musician, which might tempt a congregation to put the musician on a pedestal, or lead a musician to remain aloof. Even though some of these musicians are deserving of professional acclaim from a secular point of view, they maintain a pastoral relationship with the congregation. In doing so, they enhance the ability of the parishioners to participate as full partners in liturgy as the work of the people.

Music for a Lifetime

What we heard again and again from members of the congregations we studied was how important music is to their worship and how much they look forward to it each week. Congregations value music as a means of carrying prayer and praise, as a way of feeling closer to God. The communal aspect of music-making is important too. We learned from the congregation in chapter 9 that growing older as a congregation means that what members value most is their worship together. Worship is their corporate reason for being. Life's milestones—baptisms, marriages, funerals—are marked in the church. These important occasions are accompanied by music and texts that become vital to personal and communal faith journeys. Music makes the theology of these occasions memorable. Particular hymns become lifelong companions for members of the congregations, recurring at milestones for the church and families.

The development of a unique core repertoire of music used in worship is important to each congregation's identity. This repertoire serves it well not only for formal worship, but also in other congregational gatherings. Confidence with this body of hymnody allows church members to explore new hymns, which many do with vigor. All the congregations move forward by building on the traditions that are part of their own community of faith. New ideas spring from what they already know. Their past informs their future and gives coherence to their journey together.

Resources and Excellence

Despite the reputation of all these congregations for their music programs, none is financed by a large endowment or has access to unlimited resources. Granted, several have fairly significant budgets, but none is excessive. Some could even be considered meager.

The evidence from this study leads us to conclude that there is not necessarily a correlation between high-quality music and resources. Rather, there is a correlation between quality and *people.* It is the leaders and people in the congregation, perhaps those in the choir or church members who appreciate the lay musicians, that provide resources so that high-quality music in worship is possible. Sometimes the pastor knows someone in the congregation who would enjoy giving an instrument to the church. Or the opportunity to secure a good piano causes parishioners to line up with their checkbooks after mass to make sure it will happen. Perhaps a talented musician in the community or in the congregation is identified, and the money is made available so that the person can be hired. If brass players are needed for Easter, a special gift makes securing their services possible. If an extra rehearsal is required to make certain the music for the first Sunday in Advent is prepared, the volunteer musicians give extra time. In short, when the congregation understands the importance of music for liturgy and knows that those making the music are committed to excellence, the resources are found for the best possible offering.

Adherence to Vatican II Criteria

While each music program is unique to its site, two threads are common to all the sites. First, the music programs have found a niche within the history and traditions of the church and congregation, and they stay within that niche. They do not try to be all things to all people. Second, the focus of the music is on the worship of God.

Article 112 in chapter VI from the *Constitution on the Sacred Liturgy* describes how the leaders of these music programs think regarding music in worship:

> The musical tradition of the universal Church is a treasure of inestimable value, greater even than that of any other art. The main reason for this preeminence is that, as sacred song closely bound to the text, it forms a necessary or integral part of the solemn liturgy.[3]

The clergy and musicians of these local churches, without exception, take these words to heart as they carefully plan week after week, year after year, the liturgies that enable their congregations to worship through song.

Clergy and musicians in this study begin their planning of worship with the readings from Scripture for the day, most often following the Revised Common Lectionary (the exception being one Presbyterian church, where the pastor occasionally uses a sermon series). Such Scripture selections determine the focus and nature of worship. Next, appropriate denominational liturgical materials are consulted for musical planning. The stage is set for music to be an integral part of the liturgy.

How each team implements the next steps to ensure that music becomes integral to the liturgy differs according to the gifts of clergy and musicians, their availability to each other for planning, and the abilities and knowledge of the congregation and the other musicians who lead in worship. What is non-negotiable for these worship leaders is the flow of liturgy, Scripture readings, and music that form a unified whole for the assembled worshipers.

Article 14 in chapter 1 from the *Constitution on the Sacred Liturgy* provides the impetus for these leaders to consider the congregation to be a vital part of worship:

The Church earnestly desires that all the faithful be led to that full, conscious, and active participation in liturgical celebrations called for by the very nature of the liturgy.[4]

All the churches embraced this value, but implementation varied somewhat. This study uncovered a multitude of ways to define participation. Congregations with some of the most robust singing in the pews have some of the strongest choirs and the largest numbers of church members involved in musical groups. These musical groups, however, are viewed not as performance entities but as participants in corporate worship. A natural flow exists between professional musicians, those with some training, and those with no training at all who participate fully in the music of worship. What is most important is that all participate.

The Catholic cathedral renovated its entire worship space to facilitate the participation of the people. The small inner-city Presbyterian congregation uses stanzas of hymns to create a liturgy the people can sing easily. The Episcopal parish musician in the Midwest introduces new service music in church-school classes, so that a significant contingent in the congregation will know it. The urban Catholic parish in the upper Midwest uses tunes familiar to the congregation, so that worshipers will feel confident in their singing. The organist at the urban Presbyterian church spends a significant portion of her practice time thinking about how to express in sound the texts of hymns through organ registration and alternate harmonizations, so the congregation will be led to sing them with full theological understanding. The musician in the New England Episcopal parish helps the members of the congregation to write their own settings of psalms for the community to sing.

The methods may differ, but the goal is the same: the full, conscious, and active participation of the people in singing their worship.

Pinnacle

CHAPTER 11

Characteristics of
Special Note

A STUDY SUCH AS THIS ENCOURAGES ONE TO DREAM about ideal environments for music in worship. More than a few pieces of that dream are reality in the congregations we studied. The good news suggested by this study is that all congregations can exercise the kind of thoughtfulness, insight, and wisdom that have enabled these congregations to build lasting music programs. They have used what is available to them to best advantage. More than anything else, their faithfulness to God, resourcefulness, and commitment to excellence define their success. This chapter lifts up notable characteristics or practices unique to one or more congregations and links them to others, past and present.

Striving for the Best

In 2003, British author Adam Nicolson gave us *God's Secretaries: The Making of the King James Bible.*[1] Nicolson explores how the process of creating this Bible translation contributed to its continuing use from 1611 to the present. King James sought the best scholars, theologians, poets, translators, historians, linguists, and writers he could find to create a Bible that has served English-speaking Christians for centuries. The compilation of the King James Bible is perhaps not all that different from what the clergy and musicians in our study and many others do in miniature as they plan worship week after week, using the best gifts of the people in their congregations and the resources at hand. Well trained, thoughtful theologians and musicians seek the best vehicles for the worship of the people they serve—vehicles of lasting strength that will carry the depth of prayer and praise required for authentic worship. They seek the best for that place and time. What does this "best" look like?

1. *Our best is the accumulated wisdom of the gifted people in our midst.* We do our best when we identify those people who are most gifted musically to lead and to discern musical gifts in others. We are the strongest community of faith when we tap the expertise in our midst for the betterment of the entire community. We take seriously the mandate of 1 Corinthians 12 to uncover "many gifts but one spirit," using the best of our individual gifts for our common purpose.

2. *Our best is the accumulated wisdom from the fields of both theology and music.* The institutional church historically has valued theology and provided for the accumulation of theological knowledge and the training of theologians. In contrast, musical knowledge and training in church music have been haphazard at best, with primary responsibility often falling to congregations. When asked how to find a musician for a church, wise congregations ask, "Who is the best musician we can find?" They look for the best musician with faith commitments and a passion for using musical gifts for worship. A well-trained professional musician with the tools and resources needed for church music can gain access to the rich treasure of the accumulated history of music of the Christian faith, as well as incorporate new and authentic musical vehicles for worship. Just as the church values education for its ministers, these congregations acknowledge the necessity of competent musical leadership for worship. Further, they have found pastors who work with musicians to integrate music with theology for worship.

3. *Our best is a congregation equipped to fulfill its task in worship.* These congregations embrace liturgy as the work of the people and set about to do their work. In his book *Congregations in America,*[2] Mark Chaves, Duke University professor of sociology of religion, demonstrates that at least twenty minutes of a seventy-minute worship service involve music. Thus, a third of an average worship service relies on worshipers' being able to participate in music in the same way they interpret the spoken word or read the words of a text in liturgy. Congregations that embrace liturgy as the work of the people also equip their people to participate in the musical offerings of worship.

4. *Our best is the development of a repertoire of music within a congregation that has lasting value over the years, music that provides nourishment for the Christian journey.* Just as Scripture becomes a primary reference for a Christian, the music that carries our theology becomes an important vehicle, and as Luther might say, is secondary only to the Scripture itself. Music engages mind, emotion, and body, and helps us to retain theological truths. The more worthy the vehicle is musically, theologically, and liturgically, the greater capacity it will have to carry the deeper elements of our faith and the more lasting it will be. These congregations treasure their repertoire, teach it to new generations, and celebrate its use in their worship experiences.

5. *Our best is the development of leaders of music for future generations.* These congregations take the responsibility to identify future music and worship leaders in childhood and mentor them through their developmental and educational years. Spiritual and musical development is a process that cannot be accomplished overnight. It takes years of persistent nurture, education, and reflection to produce the kinds of leaders who are most effective. It is important to start as early as possible. As stewards of their heritage, these congregations take responsibility to provide for the future, too.

Commitment to Education

Congregations that embrace liturgy as the work of the people, including those studied here, have a commitment to education. This includes but is not limited to children. Children's choirs, after-school programming, opportunities for singing or playing instruments in worship, musical immersion in Sunday school classes, scholarship programs—whatever the means, youth are encouraged to learn the music of the church and to incorporate it in their faith development. Adult education is considered equally important. Education is provided through adult education classes, newsletters, special events, and brief rehearsals before worship. When new music is introduced as part of worship, it is done carefully. What is it that the congregation already knows? How can we build on that to introduce the new? How can we use those gifted in music (choir, soloists, organist, other instrumentalists) to introduce the new music, so that when the worshipers are asked to sing they will be successful? Care is always given to *what* the congregation is asked to sing. Are the music and text worthy to put into the people's mouths? Will it be apparent *why* they are being asked to sing this particular music at this place in the liturgy?

The Presbyterian church in a university town (chapter 7) has had a commitment since the 1940s to fund a scholarship program for students who become part of the congregation. They learn how to be church musicians, and the congregation learns about music by following the lives of these young people as they train to become professional musicians. The investment is a two-way street: the congregation gives the scholarships to students to aid them in their education, and the congregation receives their gifts of music in worship in return, as well as an understanding of how the field of music and musicians function. The students learn how church music is done at a high standard, and many of them go on to professional music careers, some into church music careers. The congregation follows their careers and learns what it means to be a music professional who influences the decisions that are made about music in the congregation.

The Episcopal parish church in a Midwest suburb (chapter 4) explores sacred music of the past and appropriates it for current liturgies. The volunteer choir from the congregation learns the primary content of these masterworks for the liturgical offering. Classes for the congregation precede the rendering of the masterwork, so that congregants are prepared to participate in the work as a liturgy rather than a performance. The children's choirs sing the chorales for the liturgy, thereby participating fully in the worship with the congregation. While most churches would consider these masterworks "performance literature," this congregation has found a way to dip into treasures of the past and bring them into a meaningful worship experience.

In addition to the Episcopal cathedral choir school that serves a diverse neighborhood, another Episcopal parish church in the Northeast (chapter 5) embraces the ethnic diversity of its congregation, using music with texts in languages from all over the world. The Catholic cathedral in the Northwest (chapter 1) uses music from the cathedrals of immigrant worshipers' countries of origin, a gift from parishioners who have brought ethnic traditions from other places in the world. These congregations are learning music from throughout the Christian church, along with the musical skills required to sing it and the theological understanding that accompanies it.

Various means for musical education exist beyond the local congregation, and the musicians in this study use these resources themselves and provide access for members of their congregations. Organizations such as the Royal School of Church Music in America (Anglican), American Federation Pueri Cantores (Catholic), and Choristers Guild (Protestant) offer resources for the training of children. Denominational music organizations such as the National Association of Pastoral Musicians, the Association of Anglican Musicians, and the Presbyterian

Association of Musicians (representing the denominations of the churches of this study) also provide resources for church musicians. But these efforts often operate in an unofficial capacity outside the institutional church or on the fringes within it. Music of the church is hardly an institutional priority within denominational governance structures, church schools, and seminaries, and is often an afterthought. Ultimately, the local congregation retains the final responsibility for music education in the church.

Clergy-Musicians

In an era when specialization is prized and education is offered in narrowly defined disciplines, five of our nine clergy have specialized training in music. Though this training is clearly not a requirement for their successfully administering a music program or providing meaningful music in liturgy, each of these five clergy gives unusual gifts to the congregations and musicians he or she serves.

The music training of two of the Catholic priests gives special meaning to the parishioners when they celebrate the Eucharist. The priests' comfort in singing the parts of the liturgy invites ease in the response from the congregation. Because the priests sing with confidence, the parishioners respond without hesitation, giving themselves to the words of the liturgy without fear of the mechanics of singing. Congregations respond similarly to the two musically trained Presbyterian pastors, one of whom regularly serves as cantor for the psalms, and the other who leads brief hymn responses for the congregation.

In addition, clergy who know at least something about music enjoy camaraderie with the musicians, see them as colleagues in a common task, can affirm their musical gifts, and empower them to use these gifts in creative and unusual ways. These clergy know how to ask good questions, suggest alternatives, and give theological input in ways understood by the musicians. They also exercise their authority for worship in the best possible way, that of eliciting effective music for worship from highly trained and capable musicians.

These musically literate clergy from our study join the ranks of Jesuit priest Joseph Gelineau (1920–2008) and Congregational minister Erik Routley (1917–1982), to whom all of us who have read their writings are indebted for their commitment toward a deeper understanding of music in worship. Father Gelineau articulated his theology of music both in his writings and in his musical settings of the liturgy and psalms. Routley left us with hymns and books on theology and music. Both influenced untold numbers of clergy and musicians during their lifetimes and continue to do so through the legacies they gave. Of course, many more could be named, including Lutheran musician and pastor Paul Westermeyer and United Methodist scholar Don Saliers, who continue to enrich our worship practices.

Although the clergy in our sites may be unusual and notable, what is consistent and important to remember from their examples and others like them is that they respect and appreciate the role of music in worship and work with their musicians in partnership. A superior music education cannot substitute for a theology of music in worship and collegial working relationships.

Musician-Theologians

Scholar and musician Quentin Faulkner, formerly of the University of Nebraska, Lincoln, often remarks that church musicians are valued foremost according to the quality of their musicianship. Good musicians can acquire the skills and knowledge to become good *church* musicians. Formal study of theology can happen later. But fundamental musicianship is a prerequisite and takes a long time to learn.

Becoming a musician cannot begin as an adult, or rarely even as a teenager. Music education is the gradual development of a skill nurtured in childhood and perfected through professional study. The musicians at the Catholic cathedral in the Pacific Northwest (chapter 1) and the Episcopal congregation in a Midwest suburb (chapter 4) are notable for their uncanny ability to draw from an amazing repertoire of music in the service of the liturgy. This ability is not accidental. Both musicians were formed in Protestant, nonliturgical settings where congregational hymn singing was of vital importance. Neither was exposed to sophisticated theology in his early years, yet both were thoroughly engaged in Sunday school and attended worship regularly. Both were involved in the making of music in the church at an early age, however, exploring a natural musical curiosity within the context of the church. Both were encouraged to pursue formal music study and completed advanced professional training, albeit not theological training. They were bent on becoming superb *musicians,* and this process included the church. Although it happened at different times and in different ways, both explored theology and liturgy as they related to the making of excellent music because their integrity demanded it. Their faith development and their musical development were parallel. When they realized that their calling in the church was as much a theological task as a musical one, they sought guidance from the clergy with whom they worked and read extensively in theology. Their commitments required that they offer a product of both theological and musical excellence.

In addition, both these musicians have the ability to make excellent music available to those who are not necessarily trained musicians but who come to worship through music. These superb musicians have mastered theology and liturgy, allowing them to draw as needed and as appropriate from the vast musical resources of the historical church, as well as to select the best from recently composed music, to give expression to the faith of today's worshipers. The cathedral musician is adept at finding ways of incorporating service music from the many ethnic backgrounds of the parishioners he serves. The Episcopal musician opens masterworks of the past to give fresh liturgical vehicles to his congregation. Their drive to become the best musicians they could be also led them to an understanding of theology and liturgy. In serving the church, they quickly determined that they could not separate music and theology. Their understanding of music and liturgy becomes the basis for serving parishioners effectively in their individual contexts.

An example in another setting is Gail Walton (1954–2010), a colleague and director of music at the Basilica of the Sacred Heart at the University of Notre Dame until her untimely death. Raised in Evangelical United Brethren and Methodist churches, educated at Westminster Choir College and Eastman School of Music, Walton worked with clergy at Notre Dame who were informed by the best liturgical scholarship following Vatican II. She drew upon her substantial musicianship and knowledge of church music to create liturgies of theological depth and musical excellence. Yet she would often say, for the congregation gathered at the basilica, "Every Sunday is Easter." That is, she would encounter a new group of visitors to the campus each Sunday for whom this would be the culmination of a liturgical pilgrimage, and of whom she could assume no prior musical knowledge. She had to create music for liturgy that was both excellent and accessible day after day, week after week. That she did. Hal Hopson is a Presbyterian composer with superb musical skills, informed theological depth and insight, and an intuitive ability to write music that choirs, cantors, and congregations can voice for worship. Richard Proulx (1937–2010) among the Catholic composers and Paul Manz (1919–2009) of Lutheran ranks also had this ability.

An interesting fact about seven of the nine sites in the study, and about all but Richard Proulx in the examples above, is that these musicians were formed in Protestant settings where congregational singing was an important part of their faith formation. They understood "full, active, and conscious participation" through hymn singing long before it became a theological concept for them. Giving voice to their faith through song was as natural as eating and breathing. The experience came first, and the intellectual understanding developed later. For musicians, theological training could come later. Early musical training, church attendance, and faith experience were crucial.

These are but a few examples of musicians who combine musical talent, education, and faith in unusual and creative ways to give musical vehicles for prayer and praise. They may have begun as musicians who set out to become the best musicians they could be, but they soon discovered that church music had to have theological depth if worshipers were to voice their prayers through music. The musicians in the study and the additional examples all came to an intellectual theological understanding of music in worship *after* their musical development was well under way.

A Notable Music Program Drives a Mission

All the congregations of this study have music programs that profoundly shape and nurture them. But one congregation has empowered the music program to change the nature of the congregation at a point when it is redefining its mission. The Episcopal cathedral on the East Coast (chapter 6) has committed itself to a choir school that drives the mission of the congregation. While the cathedral historically has had a choir school, the newly defined choir school is responsive to the needs of the changing neighborhood in ways that engage and serve. It challenges and stretches members to grow in new ways, to use resources creatively, and to expand their vision for what the cathedral is meant to be at this time in its history. The cathedral is transforming itself and its neighborhood, though not without some growing pains. The transformation is happening with a commitment to excellence consistent with the tradition of Episcopal music and liturgy. The members and the parents of children in the choir school are committed to the well-being and growth of the children that unite their efforts. The gifts of these children to worship cannot be negated. They propel the congregation forward and bring vitality to a congregation that had lost focus.

Of the three Christian traditions in the study—Catholic, Episcopal, and Presbyterian—the Episcopalians have the longest history of combining liturgy with music in the English language and the most established pedagogy for training children in choir schools. The English anthem based on Scripture has developed to serve the liturgy specifically, as have multiple settings of service music. The repertoire is rich and deep. Now leaders of this cathedral must think hard about how to serve an ethnically and economically diverse population, a constituency that may not relate easily to this repertoire. Granted, a music education, which the choir school can offer, will give access to the traditional repertoire. But this congregation is now finding ways to build on its tradition to expand repertoire and include traditions from the ethnic backgrounds of its newest parishioners. It is faithful to its past and also to its present, rewriting its mission in vibrant new ways.

While most congregations will not find themselves in a situation where such profound changes will be driven by a music program, it is important to realize that music can be a positive agent of change. The history of music is as old as the Christian church. Music can move the church forward, and the church should not hesitate to activate the musical resources of our history to do so.

Spaces of Note

Three churches made major investments in facility renovations that have driven their worship in new directions and have changed the nature of their congregations.

The Catholic cathedral in the Northwest (chapter 1) decided to focus its energy and resources on renovating the interior space to create an aesthetically and acoustically beautiful environment for liturgy. Careful planning and major investment in reorganizing the space and locating an additional organ to support congregational singing transformed the worship experience. The space became more welcoming, the liturgical experience refreshingly different. The result has been growth in the numbers of parishioners coming to the cathedral as well as increased participation in the liturgy.

Parishioners of the urban neighborhood Presbyterian church (chapter 8) spent a long while determining the acoustics and the aesthetic they wanted in the sanctuary. Carpeting was a major issue. The sanctuary carpeting was removed and replaced with ceramic tile, and the organ was moved to the chancel. When they finally renovated the space, they also made a major investment in rehearsal space for the music programs. The additional rehearsal spaces have allowed for a decided increase in the number of participants in the music programs. Church membership has grown, and the hymn singing of the congregation has improved markedly.

The Episcopal parish church (chapter 4) renovated its rectangular nave, adding two wide transepts and moving the altar to the center to create a sense of worshiping "in the round." The result is a welcoming, uncluttered visual and acoustical environment that has enlivened worship and music participation. A side benefit of the restoration process was the addition of a fine piano and a portative organ, which were used while the organ was away in England for restoration, giving more variety to musical expression in the space.

In both the Catholic and Presbyterian sites, investment in renovation of the worship space had two striking outcomes: participation in worship increased visibly, and growth in the number of people coming regularly to worship was significant. The Episcopal site renovation has allowed the improved space to be used for more vital music in worship and also for events designed for outreach into the community.

The requirements for good worship spaces are unlike those of other public spaces where the acoustic needs can be more specific, such as concert halls built only for music performance or a stage or lecture hall that needs only amplification for speakers. When designing and appointing space, churches must consider speaking, the offerings of musical groups, congregational singing, and the placement of accompanying instruments. Few architects are prepared to address these multiple demands or know how to work with acousticians to accomplish the goals of vital worship, and wise congregations will search to find the few.

If one measures priority by resources, hiring of personnel, educational opportunity, and a place at the table when important decisions are made, it is clear that music is not a high priority in the broader church. It is also apparent that the inspiration, vision, and hard work of the people in a congregation can provide for music that gives life-changing opportunities for a worshiping community. When the work of the people is done well, the music soars, the prayer and praise are complete, and worshipers are readied to do their work in the world.

With Clouds

CHAPTER 12

Implications for the Future

COMPLETING THIS PROJECT LEAVES ALL SORTS OF QUES-
TIONS unanswered. How could these models be replicated?
What implications do these findings have for how we view
church music? How can we shape a better future for worship
because of what we have learned? The findings have profound
implications for the training of clergy and musicians and for
how we view the role of congregations in worship and music.
But first, we must acknowledge that music matters. If there is
anything this study says about these congregations, it is that
music matters a great deal to them.

Acknowledging Music alongside Theology

The church acknowledges the knowledge and practice of theology as important to the function of the Christian church and
trains its clergy accordingly. Unlike clergy, however, musicians
rarely have formal training in theology. Likewise, while music
has accompanied Christian worship from earliest times, the
education and training of clergy in music has not been consistent. The body of Christian music is remarkable in its depth and
breadth, containing some of the finest treasures in all of music
literature. The Christian church has a wealth of repertoire from

which current Christians can choose to enrich present-day worship. If clergy and musicians were crossed-trained to access these treasures, Christian worship could be transformed, as these nine models demonstrate.

The clergy in this study did not receive training in music as part of their seminary educations, nor did the musicians receive training in theology as part of their formal training. Yet each understood the importance of training in the other's field and sought it on their own. The congregations of this study acknowledge the music of the church as a treasure and delve into it deeply. They provide a model for how the broader church could think about music in worship, and for how musicians and clergy should be prepared to lead congregations in worship. They show us what is possible.

Church musicians have been engaged in music-making for hundreds of years, working alongside clergy to give voice to the prayers of the people through song. These musicians set Scripture to music in myriad ways for choirs and congregations and have developed a performance practice (an appropriate and effective means of offering music in worship) that gives depth and meaning to liturgy for worshipers today. The churches of this study acknowledge the vital role of church musicians and support them wholeheartedly.

But to have impact for the broader church, music must be acknowledged in its own right. Music is a field of endeavor, just like theology, with its own history, practice, and rules of engagement. In many ways the same rules that define good music-making elsewhere in our society define good music in worship. The churches in the study want good music for worship; they serve as models for the broader church. They attend to the professional qualifications of their musicians just as they do their clergy and provide resources for the music program as a necessary part of the functioning of their church. They can do no less. It is part of the practice of their faith. What is also apparent is that these are congregationally driven mandates rather than standards set by their denominations or other outside entities. Yet they do not shrink from outside evaluations of their music-making, whether sacred or secular.

Singing faithfully involves the big picture; and prepared, educated, wise leaders know how music is intertwined with faithful worship. Educated leaders will understand the dual roles of music and theology and how each contributes to the music of worship. Educated musicians will unleash and encourage the abilities of the congregation, so that the people's voices and gifts empower communal praise and prayer. Wise clergy will work closely with such musicians to find the best music to accompany biblical texts for the day, creating worship that addresses the whole person—heart, mind, and body.

Once music and theology are acknowledged as companion disciplines necessary for coherent worship, the next step is to prepare leaders to work in this interdisciplinary field.

Music Training for Clergy

The clergy in this study had little if any training in music as part of their seminary study or ordination requirements. Their training in music happened in the church experiences of their childhoods, for most of them beginning in children's choirs, and several studied music formally. Yet one of the older clergy in the study remarked that he thought his generation might be the last to be formed in these ways. He laments that worship driven by a popular-culture, marketplace mentality is missing all the rich resources of the past. We know that today's seminarians do not necessarily come to seminary with lifelong formation in the church, sometimes choosing pastoral work after a career in another field or in the wake of a religious experience. When seminarians (1) do not have early musical and liturgical formation grounded in biblical and historical Christian traditions, (2) have no training in music and liturgy as part of seminary curricula, and (3) enter parish work charged with the responsibility for music and worship for local congregations without adequate preparation, they are not equipped for the task of leading worship. A review of statistics gathered by the Association of Theological Schools (ATS), the accrediting agency for seminaries in the United States and Canada, raises additional questions about graduating seminarians' capacity to work with music and musicians. Twelve of the 263 ATS-accredited schools offer degrees in church music. Only twenty-six of the remaining 251 institutions have full-time music faculty positions. This means that seminaries are training few church musicians[1] and that the vast majority of clergy are trained in the absence of professional musicians. The first time these pastors may encounter a musician in a professional capacity is in their first parish assignment.

Correcting this situation will require efforts from more than one of the constituencies involved in preparing and nurturing clergy. First, seminaries would do well to screen their candidates for worship and music formation, as well as for music skills needed to function as a pastoral leader. Then, training in seminary or as part of continuing education in hymnology, theology of music in worship, psalm singing, and service music can accompany the study of liturgy and its practice. Judicatory and denominational bodies that oversee ordination requirements should include competence in music and worship as part of preparation for service to the church. Finally, congregations can take responsibility early on for the education of children, youth, and adults in worship and music as part of the Christian education and catechism teaching for Christian discipleship, assuring not only that future Christian leaders are trained from childhood but also that laypeople are prepared to do their work.

Theological Training for Musicians

Some of the musicians in the study had church music degrees, but most did not, relying instead on their secular professional music training and on-the-job theological training. In all cases, the musicians were either self-motivated or worked with clergy who understood the nature of music and worship and who engaged the musicians in reflection about the theology of musical decisions. How can musicians without these unusual circumstances acquire basic theological preparation for their task, and further, how will denominational differences be addressed when they move across faith traditions? Most of these musicians were not professionally prepared as *church* musicians. Motivated by personal integrity, supported by mentors, and influenced by their working environments, they learned how to become church musicians. What happens when musicians are not motivated to prepare themselves theologically, perhaps viewing the church primarily as an excellent place to perform? Or what happens when they adopt a philosophy of church music that does not take into account its liturgical function, such as, for example, "All music is a gift of God, and its performance can be celebrated as worship"? Or perhaps they might have a more pietistic approach: "God gave me this song that I would like you to sing as part of our worship today," regardless of whether it fits the context?

A survey of institutions accredited by the National Association of Schools of Music (NASM) indicates there are seventy-four degree programs in either church or sacred music in the United States. Only two of these programs are situated in a seminary or school of theology. The NASM requirements specify what music skills are required for the practice of music in religious settings but are silent where theological knowledge and reflection are concerned. If clergy cannot discuss a theology of liturgical music or the musician is not open to such conversation, coherent worship music is unlikely to happen. Then, the best one can hope for is that good sacred music will coexist with the spoken word in worship, regardless of whether the two relate.

As we have seen in the nine models of this study, the alternatives are worth the pursuit. Coherent worship is the result when musicians apply theological principles in the practice of music in worship. As our study indicates, local congregations can do much to mentor future church musicians. Providing professional training in seminaries for musicians alongside clergy would be the optimal scenario. Short of that, university sacred music programs would do well to partner with seminaries for collaborative ventures in which music students could have ongoing practical experience working with seminarians in planning and leading worship services. Seminaries also could initiate continuing education programs that would involve teams of clergy and musicians in training. Denominations could (and some already do) provide certification programs to train musicians to serve their churches. Until these more institutional approaches are launched, congregations can make sure their musicians have funding for theological education opportunities that do exist, as well as access to resources for liturgical music.

The Church Music Institute, founded in 2006, is committed to the education of worship and music leaders and to providing access to the best resources available for these leaders. (See www.churchmusicinstitute.org.)

For both clergy and musicians preparing for leadership in the church, accrediting agencies such as the Association for Theological Schools and the National Association of Schools of Music would do well to consider the interdisciplinary nature of church music and begin to develop standards for the education of leaders in their respective fields. Training for church music leadership is fractured, and efforts from these accrediting agencies that are charged with determining educational standards would alert constituencies to its importance.

Preparing the
Congregation for Its Participation

The word *liturgy* has its roots in the Greek word *leitourgia,* which combines the words for *work* and *people.* "Liturgical" describes communal Christian worship that is participatory. Thus, if we

speak of Christian worship or liturgy, we are speaking about the
work of the people. What do the people need to participate fully
in worship? What do people need to know to sing God's song
faithfully? Granted, participation can be defined as listening or
speaking, but singing requires full body involvement and hence
has been a primary means of communal participation. Don Saliers says:

> The gathering of a Christian community to sing praises to
> God seems such a simple act, and it has been going on for
> nearly two millennia. But we should not take this practice
> for granted. It needs to be learned and nurtured and taught.
> And it needs to keep developing, as it has done through the
> centuries and continues to do today.[2]

Paul Westermeyer defines the *cantor* as the leader of the *people's
song*.[3] The song belongs to the people. The task of the cantor,
then, is to develop the *voice* of the congregation. In our era of
performers and audiences, of microphones and speakers, of
stages and spotlights, the idea that the gathered body of Christians does the work of worship may sound a bit odd. Yet that
is precisely the foundation of Christian worship, explained by
Søren Kierkegaard as a drama with congregation as actors, leaders as prompters, and God as the audience. It is a concept also
affirmed by Vatican II documents:

> The Church earnestly desires that all the faithful be led to
> that full, conscious, and active participation in liturgical
> celebrations called for by the very nature of the liturgy. Such
> participation by the Christian people as "a chosen race, a royal
> priesthood, a holy nation, God's own people" is their right and
> duty by reason of their baptism."[4]

Today's church lives in a culture where we are more likely to
listen to music than to sing or play it. This state of affairs has
profound implications for a church whose worship has been

sung for all of its history. If we value this head, body, and heart experience of worship, congregations need ways to build their singing capacity. If we ignore this value, we not only lose hundreds of years of worship practice and tradition that have made the faith real to worshipers since Old Testament times, but we also lose the capacity for congregations to do their work through song, in the one way that allows head, heart, and body together to offer praise and prayer to God.

So how can a congregation and its leaders go about claiming the rights and performing the duties of their baptism through the vehicle of music?

1. *Congregations can purposefully master a broad and deep repertoire of hymnody and service music that will reside in the memory of the community.* Granted, this effort will be different for every congregation and will change over time. Clergy and music leaders can help the congregation determine this repertoire, but ultimately it belongs to the congregation. Every congregation is situated in a particular cultural and ethnic context and has its own musical gifts. Experience shows that the life of a hymnal is about twenty years. Yet a succession of hymnals in any one denomination will share a surprising number of the same hymns, as will the hymnals across a variety of denominations, so these often serve as a starting place. Familiar music can form a basis for an ongoing repertoire and set a standard for other music to be added to the collection. After a basic repertoire is mastered, confidence will allow the exploration of a wealth of new music to enhance and enrich worship.

2. *Leaders can teach the congregation the art of singing.* Singing is a physical act requiring breath and movement. Understanding how the body produces sound and reading music are fundamental to singing. Sophisticated knowledge is not necessary, but following the movement of pitches and having some understanding of simple note values helps. Perhaps a twenty-first-century equivalent of the early American singing schools could be initiated. Bulletin notes, Sunday school classes, adult education offerings—all are possibilities for such education.

3. *Stewards of church facilities can provide the acoustic environment for singing.* Perhaps the greatest deterrent to good congregational singing is a dead acoustical environment. Hard surfaces create the best sound environment for singing, allowing voices to blend easily so that no individual voices sound alone. Even in acoustically dead environments, simple remedies can help, such as painting sound-absorbent acoustical tile or removing carpet.

4. *Musicians can accompany with sensitivity.* Instrumentalists who play too loudly or do not "breathe" with singers will discourage singing. Good accompaniment facilitates but does not dominate the "voice of the people," helping the people listen to one another rather than to the accompaniment.

5. *Leaders can seek out capable musicians in the congregation to enrich the song.* Choirs, instrumentalists, children, and anyone with special musical gifts can add enormously to the song of the people. When woven carefully into the fabric of the music of worship, they lend "many gifts but one spirit." When given the opportunity to contribute to a verse of a hymn, a descant, a prelude, or an offertory, individual musicians reflect the tapestry of the congregation and give cause for celebration and thanksgiving.

Building the capacity of the congregation to offer its praise and prayer in song increases worshipers' participation in ways that nothing else can. It not only engages many aspects of the individual but also connects many individuals in ways that create community. When communal music-making is done with skill and creativity, beauty and transcendence result, making possible an encounter with God.

Creating Harmonious Relationships

For those interested in music and worship with active congregational participation, led by a strong partnership of clergy and music leaders, this study suggests factors that can contribute to an environment where such participatory worship can flourish. Of

primary importance are leaders with characteristics of servanthood, who have a confidence in their own preparation, gifts, and
calling that allows them to affirm the gifts of others. Awareness
of pitfalls in collaborative endeavors is also helpful. If factors that
promote greater harmony in the working relationships of clergy
leaders and musicians can be identified, this awareness will lead
to better relationships not only between leaders but also among
congregational members.

A potential source of conflict between leaders stems from
the fact that musicians have often served in a given congregation longer than the clergy. Clergy have professional status
within the denomination and are able (and even expected) to
move among congregations, but musicians tend to stay in one
location, sometimes for their entire careers. The long tenure of
musicians contributes to the strength and stability of church
music programs and to strong relationships with members of the
congregation. These positive attributes of a musician's longevity
in one job can become problematic when a new priest or pastor
arrives who did not hire the musician, or perhaps when one or
the other is not inclined to work collaboratively. Though the
long tenure of musicians was not a problem in any of the sites at
the time of the study, it is interesting to note that all the clergy
who mentioned conflict as an issue also worked with musicians
who have been in place significantly longer than they. The relationships of these leaders and their commitment to a common
task helped them to work through the initial transition.

Even though the longevity of a musician's employment in
one congregation did not become a serious issue in any of the
sites in the study, it is easy to see how conflict could arise in such
a situation. A long-term musician may be seen as an obstacle
to a new priest or pastor who wants to make changes in worship or music. In all three of the denominations studied, the
structural authority for music in worship clearly resides with
the clergy. But if the musicians are loved by the congregation,
their relationships with parishioners give the musicians a source

of authority outside of the official structure. Musicians are "in charge" of an important area over which the pastor is supposed to have authority but to whom the congregation does not give the power to exercise it.

Other factors precipitating conflict over music can be anticipated. Pastors who want to make changes in music may be hampered by a lack of ability to articulate the desired alterations. The musicians, and perhaps the congregation, may see the prospect of "change" as an attack on something they value highly—a cherished music program or a part of worship—even though the pastor intends something different. Without language and understanding to articulate a point of view, an objective exchange of ideas is difficult.

Pastors may not know how to deal with the strong responses music conveys to the congregation in worship. I asked one of the pastors trained in music about this phenomenon. His response: "I think all of us who preach secretly wish that our words had the power of music. If only we could understand and appreciate that power and use it in the best sense."

Musicians may not be able to explain to a pastor why certain musical traditions are important to a congregation. A musician's first language usually is that of sound rather than words, an initial barrier. Unfamiliarity with theological language is yet another barrier. Perhaps we should be surprised that many of these relationships work at all!

The examples of difficulty that surfaced as part of this study are hardly unusual—and are in fact minor in comparison to other situations. In one Presbyterian congregation, a minister abruptly replaced a musician who had been employed by the church for more than twenty years. Recently, a Catholic musician met her replacement before she knew she had been terminated. In another location, an Episcopal musician's salary was cut in half because the priest unilaterally decided that rehearsals for the musicians leading worship were unnecessary. A musician may take a church position without a sense of pastoral calling, believing it to be a fine place for music performance, and trouble then ensues when the emphasis on performance compromises the needs of worship. We have much work to do to identify norms for professional roles in church music leadership, but the examples of these nine sites are a good start.

The clergy and musicians in this study avoided the pitfalls cited above because they are clear about their callings, deeply respect their colleagues and parishioners, see themselves as learners in the task of leading, and above all, are servant leaders. Theirs was an attitude of submission to the Scriptures, liturgy, and music as structures within which they sought to be creative, prayerfully considering how to find the most excellent vehicles for the worship of God. Authority, ego, and control were subservient to greater goals. Harmonious relationships resulted. Their congregations were the recipients of this goodwill in creative working relationships with their leaders and with each other. Effective liturgy, the work of the people, is the real result.

Preparing Congregations to Do Their Work

Of course, the very best way to train future congregations is to begin with the children. Both spiritual and musical development require years of training and discipline, and in the church we have the opportunity to provide these effectively, since music and spirituality are ready companions. Children develop much of their ability to hear and match pitch during their early years, so learning music in early childhood is important. Although beginning as a teenager or young adult is possible, most aspiring musicians cannot make up for the early years lost to "catch up" in developing skills and musicianship. The graded choir programs and a companion curriculum to teach children hymns of the church, efforts observed in the study, are good places to begin. The musicians interviewed in this study also emphasize the importance of identifying young people with leadership gifts early and nurturing their development.

In 2006, the Knight Foundation released statistics from a study of fifteen orchestras across the U.S.[5] Though a church is hardly a symphony orchestra, the findings have application for congregations that are serious about continuing strong programs of music in worship. Both an orchestra and the church may have a repertoire that has accumulated over hundreds of years. Both attempt to transmit ideas beyond the popular and superficial, requiring education and development of their respective constituencies. Both use art forms in the pursuit of high ideals. Here are relevant conclusions from that study:

- Despite predictions of the death of classical music and its audience, there is healthy support for the art form.
- The problems of orchestras stem not from the music they play but from the ways that music is offered and sustained in their cultural context.
- An orchestra cannot be all things to all people. The mission of an orchestra needs to be clear, focused, and achievable.
- Free programming and outreach do not turn people into ticket buyers. They simply turn people into consumers of free programming.
- There is no evidence that exposure programs for children—especially the large concert-format offerings for schoolchildren—will turn them into ticket buyers as adults.
- There is growing evidence that participatory music education—primarily instrumental lessons and ensemble and choral programs—will turn children into ticket buyers later in life.[6]

The church is heir to a historical treasury of music that parallels that of orchestral music. The demise of church music has been predicted along with that of the orchestra.[7] In the church, we affirm a gospel that is nearly two thousand years old, one that always has had music associated with it. We have a repertoire of sacred and liturgical music that goes back centuries. Denominations are publishing new hymnals that include hymns from the fourth century.[8] Organs based on centuries-old designs are still being installed and maintained. (72 percent of churches in the recent Presbyterian Hymnal committee survey use organs in worship.[9])The majority of choirs are still found in churches (80 percent, according to ChorusAmerica),[10] and more live music is made in churches than in all other venues combined in our society.[11] Despite the predictions of the death of a tradition as old as the psalms, church music is still alive. This book gives nine examples of where it is working and explores why. Although our music is different from that of an orchestra, perhaps an examination of our delivery systems is due. Are we taking seriously our heritage and transmitting it to new generations in forms they can assimilate? Are we giving equal weight to spoken and musical portions of liturgy in leadership training, education, and resources?

If an orchestra cannot be all things to all people, can a church be so? In this study, the churches did not try to be all things to all people but built music programs that were linked to traditions important to their congregations. They were hardly stuck in the past, however, rather using a breadth of music that was always grounded in their particular tradition of excellence. They did not try to "attract" worshipers by offering music aimed at pleasing outsiders, but attracted outsiders because their music was authentic, meaningful, and accessible to all in the congregation. Mark Chaves, in the conclusions of his latest National Congregations Study, indicates that U.S. churches seem to be a mirror of culture rather than leading or providing an alternative to culture.[12] Is it possible that churches can be most faithful to the gospel by being authentic about their identity, providing spiritual nourishment through music and texts of depth for their communities?

Free programming offered by the orchestra required little commitment of the participants, programming they expected would continue. Likewise, we are learning that worship that is not the work of the people does not make disciples.[13] As the ancient hymn reminds us, "Christ our God to earth descendeth, our full homage to demand." The Christian life is one of commitment and discipline. To treat our music of worship with less than our commitment and discipline is to stray from discipleship.

Perhaps the next findings of the orchestral study are most important for the future of the church. What will turn our young people into "ticket buyers" for the church? How can early musical involvement in the church lay the foundation for their commitment to the church as adults? If we continue the parallel comparison with the orchestra, the answer is not only that children need to know about good worship and music. The answer is to involve them directly in participative worship and in the *making* of good music. Teach them music skills. Help them find their voices. Imprint basic hymns, psalms, and service music upon their memories. Make a place for them to lead worship. Identify the potential leaders of song early, so that they can be nurtured spiritually and musically along the way into adulthood. As Michelangelo purportedly said about a stone, "I saw the angel in the marble and carved until I set him free." We need to observe our children carefully to find and then name their gifts for the church early and joyfully.

The Role of Music in Spiritual Formation

The past few years have brought us new awareness of the power of music. We have Baby Mozart, Baby Bach, and Baby Beethoven products and their relatives, along with knowledge that music contributes to intellectual development. Neuroscientists explain that music is fundamental to our brains and that music communicates the emotions and ideas that are the building blocks of human nature. Further, Daniel Levitin argues convincingly in his book *This Is Your Brain on Music* that music is an obsession at the heart of human nature, perhaps even more fundamental to our species than language.[14] Music therapy offers healing for mind and body. Marketing experts use the suggestive nature of music to tap our purchasing instincts. Educators understand the capacity of music to help children learn facts and concepts. We watch people who have Alzheimer's and those who have suffered a stroke retain the capacity to sing and play an instrument much longer than the ability to speak words or to carry on a conversation. Music creates memory that is more lasting than words alone. Music takes us beyond the periphery of the moment to a deeper place where mystery and metaphor live happily, as Shakespeare describes:

> And this our life exempt from public haunt
> Finds tongues in trees, books in the running brooks,
> Sermons in stones and good in every thing.
> I would not change it.[15]

Music helps us to see the same idea in new ways, to find new insights, to uncover new ways of being, to love again, to express emotion otherwise unknown. It takes us into another dimension where we can live more fully. The better the music, the greater its capacity to do its work.

A good friend has said, "We are what we sing." The music we encounter in worship is important for at least two reasons: (1) we are much more likely to remember text associated with music than spoken text alone, and (2) theology cannot be carried any deeper than the capacity the music will allow. Trite music will diminish the text associated with it. High-quality music and text will be worthy of repetition and can become part of our being to be drawn from our memory many times over. Does our faith deserve any less?

Frank Burch Brown demonstrates that the message can never be separated entirely from the music that is carrying it in his paraphrase of Psalm 23 that begins "I know the Lord's my shepherd, I won't ever need a thing," and can be sung to the tune "Rudolph the Red-Nosed Reindeer." After a discussion about the integrity of using this tune to sing this text, Brown concludes that the frivolity of the tune cannot adequately express the content of Psalm 23. This is particularly obvious in the lines "Though I walk through valleys dark as death and sin, nothing there can frighten me; with your staff you're my true friend," which match metrically with the tune but hardly express the theological depth of the Scripture.[16] As Brown says, the text and tune are a mismatch. Tunes that have proven to be lasting matches with a Psalm 23 text can be found in most hymnals: CRIMOND ("The Lord's My Shepherd, I'll Not Want"), ST. COLUMBA ("The King of Love My Shepherd Is"), and RESIGNATION ("My Shepherd Will Supply My Need").

How important it is to choose music with lasting value. Granted, we cannot always know what music will last. But we do know what music from the past has lasted and can take lessons from that. We know what general rules guide good music composition. We know what constitutes singable melodies and strong harmonies. While we may not get it right every time, we can summon our best people and gifts to make the best decisions we can. Our choices matter.

When good music is linked with good texts and these are imprinted upon our memories, the process can be an important part of spiritual formation. Besides the Bible, the hymnal may be the most important collection of theological truth for any Christian. A hymnal contains the wisdom of the ages in poetic form, set to music so that it can be remembered. A hymnal is often organized by liturgical year and theological topic, so that it becomes a teaching tool about the components of the faith. Learning a good portion of these hymns will go a long way toward helping one understand how to live the Christian life.

Learning service music gives us a voice to pray and praise in worship. Some understanding of hymnody and service music opens a window to other sacred music that deepens the Christian walk.

More Research Needed

Although Mark Chaves has conducted valuable research about congregations in the United States, we know little about their worship life and even less about the role of music in their worship. Another similar study with more sites and denominational breadth could give depth and nuance to the findings of this study. The findings in regard to numerous factors are amazingly consistent across these three denominations and nine sites. New studies will explore topics that arose as part of this study, such as why collegial clergy/musician relationships are so important, the effect of early mentorship in leadership formation, the effectiveness of servant leadership styles, and the advantages of both theological and musical training for clergy and musicians.

Further, it would be fascinating to glean even more information from congregation members. In our conversations with members during site visits, we saw the influence of the congregations in their allocation of resources to support music personnel and programs. But a more formal study of congregational members would give greater insight into how they view the role of the congregation in worship and music and why they support their congregations' worship and music. We also noted the vital role music plays in the lives of churchgoers over many years and across generations, a finding especially evident in the congregation whose older members made sure their music in worship was splendid even when other activities could no longer be sustained. Why does music have such lasting value, and how can this fact be used in making decisions about music for worship? How does church music contribute to ongoing discipleship? How could new initiatives in music strengthen the church in the twenty-first century?

At the Beginning

Although music has been a part of Christian worship as long as Christians have prayed and praised, we are only beginning to realize its importance. The power of music and its impact have been understood intuitively and in practice for centuries. It is for twenty-first-century Christians to discover this treasure anew as we define our faith in this time and place, using a gift as old as faith itself. Thanks be to God for this extraordinary gift. Let the song continue.

Still

Questions for First Interview

1. What is your "job description" here? What is your responsibility in the musical life of the congregation?

2. Tell me about your interest in music and how it developed.

3. Tell me about your connection to the church. How did you come to have a vocation in the church?

4. How do you understand the place of music in the liturgy? Give me an example from your work here at [*name of church*].

5. What is your concept of a good leader?

6. What is your understanding of the role of a "professional" musician in a congregation?

7. How would you describe the function of musical leadership within the context of the ongoing faith life of a congregation?

8. Describe a time when something stood in the way of effective musical leadership.

9. Does [*name of church*] have any musical "traditions" that you've noticed in your time here? Are there characteristics that you would say are unique to the parish?

10. Is there anything else you wish to add? Remember that we will have another interview.

APPENDIX B

Questions for Second Interview

1. What are the resources for music in worship available to you in this church?

2. What are the resources for music in worship available to you in the community?

3. Which of these resources have you taken advantage of? Have you found some more valuable than others?

4. What resources would like to see developed or reclaimed from the past?

5. Who are the people that you would consider mentors in your work?

6. Where do you find nourishment for your work?

7. How do you go about planning? What is the organizational structure here? Consider both formal and informal structures in your answer.

8. What happens when "best-laid plans" break down, when administrative procedures don't work for some reason? Can you give us an example from your work here?

9. How would you describe the liturgical piety (or pieties, given multiple services) of this congregation? How does the music serve this?

10. Vatican II was a powerful "resource" for liturgical change. It espoused two values or goals for the congregation's

worship: (1) Music forms a necessary or integral part of the solemn liturgy; and (2) the liturgy promotes the full and active participation by all the people. First, do you agree that these values are important? Second, how do you implement them in your work?

Questions for Third Interview

1. How does the congregation enable you to lead?

2. How has the congregation created an environment that makes it possible for members to worship the way they do?

3. How does the congregation understand itself as a singing/worshiping community?

4. What does music mean for members as part of the ongoing life of a congregation?

5. Why is your congregation committed to high-quality music?

6. Why has your parish put money and other resources into supporting high-quality music and musicians?

Notes

PREFACE

1. See Stephen A. Marini's book *Sacred Song in America: Religion, Music and Public Culture* (Champaign: University of Illinois Press, 2003) for a detailed discussion of the role of sacred song across the United States during this time, as he presents a historical, musicological, and theoretical inquiry into the roles of religious ritual music in public culture.

2. *Constitution on the Sacred Liturgy*, 1963, chapter VI, "Sacred Music," articles 112, 114, 115, 116, 120, 121, in *The Liturgy Documents: A Parish Response*, vol. I, 3rd ed. (Chicago: Liturgy Training Publications, 1991), 30–32.

3. Marion J. Hatchett, *A Manual for Clergy and Church Musicians* (New York: Church Hymnal Corporation, 1980), 15–16.

4. *The Book of Confessions* from The Constitution of the Presbyterian Church, U.S.A., Part II, "The Ministry of Reconciliation," B. 2.

5. *The Book of Order* of the Presbyterian Church (U.S.A.), W-2.1003.

6. While using a liturgy similar to that of Catholics, Episcopalians have used music with English text for a long time. Presbyterians have structured their worship practice around the use of hymns and psalms, allowing the music to "function as liturgy" in worship. The cross-fertilization of music among these faith traditions means all three traditions will likely use some of the same music but in different ways.

7. See Diana Butler Bass, *Christianity for the Rest of Us: How the Neighborhood Church Is Transforming the Faith* (New York: HarperSanFrancisco/ HarperCollins, 2006) for a recent and more general study of congregations in the United States.

8. Paul Greenberg's comments are taken from his column "Simple Gifts" in the Arkansas Democrat-Gazette, August 9, 2009, about the exhibition of photographs of rural Arkansas churches by David R. Mann, from which these are excerpted, at the Arkansas Studies Institute in Little Rock, Arkansas

9. From the Artist's Statement accompanying the 2009 Exhibit at the Arkansas Studies Institute. David R. Mann is an adjunct professor in the art department at the University of Arkansas, Little Rock.

INTRODUCTION

1. Ernest Boyer, *Scholarship Reconsidered: Priorities of the Professoriate* (Ewing, N.J.: Carnegie Foundation of the Advancement of Teaching, 1990), 17.

2. Ibid., 18–19.

3. Ibid., 21–23.

4. Ibid, 23–24.

5. Jane Marshall, *Grace Noted* (Carol Stream, Ill.: Hope Publishing Co., 1992), 87–89.

6. Frank Burch Brown, *Good Taste, Bad Taste, and Christian Taste: Aesthetics in Religious Life* (New York: Oxford University Press, 2000), 251.

CHAPTER 10: COMMONALITIES ACROSS DENOMINATIONS AND CONTEXTS

1. *Pastoral Constitution on the Church in the Modern World,* promulgated by Pope Paul VI, December 7, 1965, Articles 3, 92.

2. Avery Dulles, S.J., *Models of the Church* (Garden City, N.Y.: Doubleday, 1974), 90.

3. *Constitution on the Sacred Liturgy,* chapter VI, "Sacred Music," art. 112.

4. Ibid., chapter II, "Promotion of Liturgical Instruction and Active Participation, art. 14.

CHAPTER 11: CHARACTERISTICS OF SPECIAL NOTE

1. Adam Nicolson, *God's Secretaries: The Making of the King James Bible* (New York: HarperCollins, 2003).

2. Mark Chaves, *Congregations in America* (Cambridge, Mass,: Harvard University Press, 2004), 169.

Chapter 12: Implications for the Future

1. According to the Association of Theological Schools 2009–2010 Graduating Student Questionnaire, 10 of 2,947 M.Div. and 2,629 non–M. Div. seminary graduates anticipated working in church music positions. See www.ats.edu/Resources/Student/Pages/GraduatingStudentQuestionnaire.

2. Don Saliers, "Singing Our Lives," in Dorothy C. Bass, ed., *Practicing Our Faith* (San Francisco: Jossey-Bass, 1997), 184.

3. Paul Westermeyer, *The Church Musician* (Minneapolis: Augsburg Fortress, 1997).

4. *Constitution on the Sacred Liturgy*, II. Promotion of Liturgical Instruction and Active Participation, 14.

5. Thomas Wolf/Wolf, Keens & Co., "Magic of Music" Final Report, *The Search for Shining Eyes: Audiences, Leadership and Change in the Symphony Orchestra Field* (Miami: John S. and James L. Knight Foundation, 2006); available for downloading at www.Knightfoundation.org/research&publications.

6. Ibid., 6.

7. William Easum, *Dancing with Dinosaurs: Ministry in a Hostile and Hurting World* (Nashville: Abingdon, 1993), 81.

8. Two familiar examples are "Let All Mortal Flesh Keep Silence" from the Liturgy of St. James and "Lord Jesus, Think on Me" by Synesius of Cyrene.

9. www.presbyterianhymnal.org/research, Summary of Results, p. 1.

10. Of 270,000 choruses nationwide, 216,000 are religious choruses, according to *The Chorus Impact Study 2009,* p. 4, available at www.chorus america.org.

11. Mark Chaves, *Congregations in America* (Boston, Mass.: Harvard University Press, 2004), 188.

12. Mark Chaves, "American Congregations at the Beginning of the 21st Century" in National Congregations Study, 2009 at Duke University, 10–11, available at www.soc.duke.edu/natcong/Docs/NCSII_report_final.pdf.

13. Greg L. Hawkins and Cally Parkinson, *Reveal: Where Are You?* (Barrington, Ill.: Willow Creek Association, August, 2007).

14. Daniel J. Levitin, *This Is Your Brain on Music: The Science of a Human Obsession* (New York: Dutton/Penguin Group, 2006). Also by the same

author, and with specific references to religion, *The World in Six Songs: How the Music Brain Created Human Nature* (New York: Penguin Group, 2008).

15. William Shakespeare, *As You Like It,* act 2, scene 1, with thanks to Arlo Duba for this reference.

16. Frank Burch Brown, "Worship Mismatch: When the Words and Music Don't Fit," *The Christian Century*, March 10, 2009, 22–25.